The
Ultimate Little
MARTINI
BOOK

RAY FOLEY

Published by Sourcebooks, Inc.
P.O. Box 4410, Naperville, Illinois 60567-4410
(630) 961-3900
Fax: (630) 961-2168
www.sourcebooks.com

Library of Congress Cataloging-in-Publication Data:

Foley, Ray.
  The ultimate little martini book / Ray Foley.
    p. cm.
  Previously published: [S.l.] : Foley Pub., c2005.
  1. Martinis. I. Title.
  TX951.F5947 2010
  641.8'74--dc22

                    2010020945

Printed and bound in Canada.
WC 10 9 8 7 6 5 4 3 2

To Jaclyn Marie and Ryan Foley, and to the other tribe, Raymond, William, and Amy.

To all the great readers of *Bartender Magazine* and www.bartender.com, and especially to all the olives, twists, and onions!

ACKNOWLEDGMENTS

To the amazing staff at Sourcebooks, especially Sara Kase for her assistance and her handling of all problems by not making them problems, but turning them into solutions. Also for getting the names of a couple of great bars in Chicago.

Peter Lynch for his foresight and for having great taste in his selection of books.

Dominique Raccah for being Dominique Raccah.

Lauren Saccone for being Lauren Saccone. Check out her blog: www.fearandloathingny. blogspot.com.

All the readers of *Bartender Magazine* and www.bartender.com, and all the bartenders in the USA!

A SHORT HISTORY OF THE ORIGINS OF THE MARTINI

Nobody is quite sure how the martini came into existence, but there are a few interesting theories...

- First made by bartender professor Jerry Thomas of San Francisco for a stranger on his way to Martinez. Thomas made it with gin, vermouth, bitters, and a dash of maraschino.

- First made by a bartender in Martinez, California, for a gold miner who struck it rich. The miner ordered champagne for the house, but there was none. The bartender offered something better—the "Martinez Special"— made with sauterne and gin. The rich miner spread the word, ordering "Martinez Specials" throughout California.

- First made at the Knickerbocker Hotel in the early 1900s by a bartender named Martini di Arma Tiggia. He is said to have mixed a martini using only dry gin and only dry vermouth.

- Named after the British army rifle called The Martini and Henry. The rifle was known for its kick, like the first sip of gin and "it" ("it" being vermouth).

- Named after Martini & Rossi vermouth, because it was first used in the drink, gin and "it," with ½ gin and ½ Martini & Rossi vermouth.

INSTRUCTIONS

- All recipes have been alphabetized for your convenience.

- All recipes have been indexed by name and by alcohol for your convenience.

- Shake, stir, swirl, strain, or whatever. It's really up to you.

- Brand names are interchangeable for the same type of alcohol. Nobody will come to hunt you down—you can use Stolichnaya, Absolut, or Skyy vodka even if the recipe calls for Skyy vodka.

- Some drinks (not many) have the same ingredients, but different brand names—pick your favorite.

- Always use the highest quality ingredients possible.

- If you have trouble finding an ingredient, omit it and go on with your life.

- If the recipe does not have measurements, use your own taste.

- French vermouth is white and dry; Italian vermouth is red and sweet.

- We do not recommend flaming a drink.

- Don't drink and drive.

- For more information, visit www.bartender.com.

- Have a great life and enjoy your martinis.

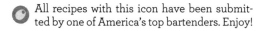 All recipes with this icon have been submitted by one of America's top bartenders. Enjoy!

Publisher's Note: This book and the recipes contained herein are intended for those of a legal drinking age. Please drink responsibly and ensure you and your guests have a designated driver when consuming alcoholic beverages.

007 Martini

Extra dry vermouth
1 oz. Gordon's Special Dry London gin
1 oz. Gordon's vodka
½ oz. Lillet
Lemon twist for garnish

Rinse a glass with extra dry vermouth. Shake with ice, and strain into the glass. Garnish with the lemon twist.

The 11 Onion Gibson

½ oz. Bombay Sapphire gin
2 drops dry vermouth
11 cocktail onions for garnish

Shake with ice, and strain into a chilled martini glass. Serve on the rocks or straight up. Garnish with the cocktail onions.

 CHARLES MCMAHAN • NEW MATAMORAS, OH

24-Karrot Martini

2 ½ oz. Ketel One vodka
Spicy baby carrot for garnish

Serve straight up or over ice. Garnish with the spicy baby carrot.

151 Martini Bacardi

3 oz. Martini & Rossi Rosso sweet vermouth
¼ oz. cranberry juice
Twist for garnish

Shake with ice, and strain into a martini glass.
Garnish with the twist.

360 Apple Tree Hugger

1 oz. 360 vodka
1 oz. sour apple schnapps
1 oz. sweet and sour mix

Shake with ice, and strain into a martini glass.

360 Double Chocolate Raspberry

2 oz. 360 Double Chocolate
1 oz. sweet and sour mix
½ oz. Agave Nectar
¼ oz. raspberry liqueur
5 Raspberries
Splash lemon-lime soda

Shake with ice, and strain into a martini glass.
Add a splash of lemon-lime soda.

1800 Carats Martini

2 ½ oz. Cuervo 1800
¼ oz. Grand Marnier
Lime squeeze

Shake with ice, and strain into a chilled martini glass.

 GATSBY • BOCA RATON, FL

1940s Classic Martini

2 ½ oz. Tanqueray gin
¼ oz. Noilly Prat
Olive for garnish

Shake with ice, and strain into a chilled martini glass. Garnish with the olive.

 CONTINENTAL CAFÉ • PHILADELPHIA, PA

1951 Martini

Splash Cointreau
2 oz. Gordon's Special Dry London gin
Anchovy-stuffed olive for garnish

Rinse the glass with Cointreau. Add gin, and garnish with the olive.

A1 Martini

2 oz. dry gin
1 oz. Grand Marnier or Cointreau
⅛ oz. grenadine
⅛ oz. lemon juice

Shake with ice, and strain into a glass.

About That Time

2 ½ oz. Alizé
Dash grenadine
Strawberry for garnish

Serve chilled in martini glass. Garnish with the strawberry.

 IRIS VOURLATOS

Absolut Hurricane Warning

1 ½ oz. Absolut vodka
1 oz. cranberry juice
1 oz. pineapple juice
Maraschino cherry for garnish

 HURRICANE RESTAURANT • PASSAGRILLE, FL

Absolut Legend Martini

2 ½ oz. Absolut vodka
¼ oz. crème de mures
¼ oz. lime juice

Shake with ice, and strain into a chilled martini glass. Serve on the rocks or straight up.

Absolut Mandrin Creamsicle

1 part Absolut Mandrin vodka
1 part white crème de cacao
Dash orange juice
Orange twist for garnish

Shake with ice, and strain into a chilled cocktail glass. Garnish with the orange twist.

Absolut Strawberry Frutini

1 part Absolut vodka
Dash dry vermouth
Dash sugar/simple syrup
2 strawberries (plus 1 for garnish)

Muddle the ingredients in a shaker. Shake with ice, and double strain into a well-chilled cocktail glass. Garnish with the strawberry.

Absolutly Fabulous Martini

1 ¼ oz. Absolut Citron vodka
1 ¼ oz. Absolut Kurant vodka
Lemon twist for garnish

Shake with ice, and strain into a chilled martini glass. Garnish with the lemon twist.

 THE MARTINI CLUB • ATLANTA, GA

Acadiana Bartender's Favorite Martini

¼ oz. sweet vermouth
Lime wedge
2 oz. Absolut Citron vodka

Shake vermouth and the lime wedge; add vodka. Shake and strain.

 STEPHANIE GUIDRY • ACADIANA'S CATFISH SHARK • LAFAYETTE, LA

Acid Rain

1 part grapefruit juice, chilled
1 part Rain vodka, chilled
Lime twist for garnish

Shake with ice, and strain into a martini glass. Garnish with the lime twist.

Acropolis Martini

1 ¾ oz. Smirnoff vodka
¼ oz. Ouzo 12
Black olive for garnish

Shake with ice, and strain into a glass. Garnish with the black olive.

Adam & Eve Martini

1 oz. Chambord
1 oz. Remy Martin VSOP
1 oz. Tanqueray gin
1 tsp. lemon juice

Shake with ice, and strain into a glass.

Addison Martini

1 ½ oz. Martini & Rossi Rosso sweet vermouth
1 oz. Bombay Sapphire gin
Maraschino cherry for garnish

Shake with ice, and strain into a glass. Garnish with the maraschino cherry.

Adios Amigos Martini

1 oz. Bombay Sapphire gin
½ oz. Bacardi rum
½ oz. brandy
½ oz. lemon juice
½ oz. Martini & Rossi Rosso sweet vermouth

Shake with ice, and strain into a glass.

Admiral Martini

1 ½ oz. Martini & Rossi vermouth
1 oz. Maker's Mark bourbon
½ oz. fresh lemon juice
Lemon twist

Shake with ice, and strain into a chilled cocktail
glass. Garnish with the lemon twist.

Adonis Cocktail

1 oz. fino sherry (Tio Pepe or La Ina)
1 oz. fresh-squeezed orange juice
1 oz. Martini & Rossi Rosso sweet vermouth
Dash Angostura bitters
Orange peel for garnish

Shake with ice, and strain into a chilled cocktail
glass. Garnish with the orange peel.

 DALE DEGROFF • EMAIL, WWW.KINGCOCKTAIL.COM

Affinity Martini

1 oz. Cutty Sark scotch
1 oz. Martini & Rossi extra dry vermouth
1 oz. Martini & Rossi Rosso sweet vermouth
2 dashes Angostura bitters
Maraschino cherry for garnish

Shake with ice, and strain into a chilled glass.
Garnish with the maraschino cherry.

Affinity #2 Martini

1 oz. Cutty Sark scotch
1 oz. dry sherry
1 oz. ruby port
2 dashes Angostura or orange bitters
Maraschino cherry for garnish

After the Frost Martini

2 oz. Bombay Sapphire gin or Finlandia vodka
1 oz. Mission Hill Grand Reserve ice wine
3 frozen Riesling grapes for garnish

Serve in a chilled martini glass set over dry ice.
Garnish with the frozen Riesling grapes.

 900 WEST IN THE CANADIAN PACIFIC HOTEL
• VANCOUVER, BC

After-Dinner Martini

2 oz. Kahlúa
¼ oz. Stolichnaya Vanil vodka
Several coffee beans for garnish

Afterglow Martini

2 parts Absolut vodka
1 part Midori melon liqueur
1 part orange juice
Dash lemon juice

Shake with ice, and strain into a glass. Serve
very cold.

Agatini

Sugar to rim
2 shots Absolut Citron vodka
Splash Chambord
Twist for garnish

Rim a martini glass with sugar. Shake with ice,
and strain into the glass. Garnish with the twist.

 PATTY NOLLETTI RESTAURANT • ROCHESTER, NY

Agnese's Goldenrod Martini

2 ½ oz. Tanqueray gin
¼ oz. Martini & Rossi extra dry vermouth
⅛ oz. Grand Marnier
Lemon rod for garnish
Orange rod for garnish

Shake with ice, and strain into a chilled martini glass. Serve on the rocks or straight up. Garnish with the lemon rod and the orange rod.

 ORSO'S • CHICAGO, IL

Air Traffic Control

1 part Courvoisier VSOP
1 part DeKuyper crème de menthe
Lemon twist for garnish

 THE WINDSOCK BAR & GRILL • SAN DIEGO, CA

Alaska Martini

2 oz. Bombay Sapphire gin
1 ½ oz. lemon juice
1 tsp. caster sugar
1 tsp. raspberry syrup or 1 tsp. crème de cassis

Shake with ice, and strain into a tall glass. Float on top raspberry syrup or crème de cassis.

Alaska Martini II

1 ½ oz. Tanqueray gin
½ oz. yellow Chartreuse

Shake with ice, and strain into a glass.

Algonquin Martini

2 oz. blended whiskey
1 oz. Martini & Rossi extra dry vermouth
1 oz. unsweetened pineapple juice

Shake with ice, and strain into a chilled cocktail
glass or serve over ice in an old-fashioned glass.

 ALGONQUIN HOTEL • NEW YORK, NY

Alizé Caribbean Martini

2 oz. Alizé
½ oz. Bacardi Limón rum
Lemon slice for garnish

Shake with ice, and strain into a martini glass.
Garnish with the lemon slice.

Alizé Martini

1 ½ oz. Alizé
½ oz. Absolut vodka
Thin slice lemon for garnish

Shake with ice, and strain into a martini glass.
Garnish with the lemon slice.

Alizé Nectar

1 ½ oz. Alizé
1 oz. grenadine
½ oz. amaretto
½ oz. Bacardi rum
½ oz. Grey Goose vodka

Shake with ice, and strain into a tall glass.

 ANDREW THOMPSON • ROCK & KATH'S SAWMILL

Alizé Passionate Martini

2 oz. Alizé
½ oz. Absolut vodka
½ oz. cranberry juice

Alizé Red Passion Martini

2 ½ oz. Alizé Red Passion
1 oz. super premium vodka
Thin slice lime for garnish

Shake with ice, and strain into a martini glass.
Garnish with the lime slice.

Alizé Tropical Martini

2 oz. Alizé
½ oz. Malibu rum
Maraschino cherry for garnish

Shake with ice, and strain into a glass. Garnish
with the maraschino cherry.

All Too Important Martini

2 ½ oz. chilled Tanqueray gin
Touch of dry vermouth (1 part to 8 parts
    Tanqueray gin)
2 olives skewered on a pick for garnish

Pour vermouth into a chilled glass, and swirl it
around. Discard the vermouth. Chill gin until
cold, and strain into the glass. Garnish with the
two olives skewered on a pick.

 JOHNNY LOVE'S • SAN FRANCISCO, CA

The All-American Martini

1 ½ oz. Glacier vodka
Dash vermouth
2 olives for garnish

Shake with ice, and strain into a chilled martini
glass. Garnish with the two olives skewered by
an American flag toothpick.

Allies Martini

1 oz. Bombay Sapphire gin
1 oz. Martini & Rossi extra dry vermouth
2 dashes kummel

Shake with ice, and strain into a chilled glass.

Aloha Martini

2 oz. Smirnoff vodka
¼ oz. Marie Brizard apricot brandy
¼ oz. pineapple juice
Pineapple wedge for garnish

Shake with ice, and strain into a glass. Garnish
with the pineapple wedge.

Alternatini Martini

Chocolate fudge to rim
3 oz. Tanqueray Sterling vodka
½ oz. white crème de cacao
Splash Martini & Rossi extra dry vermouth
Splash Martini & Rossi Rosso sweet vermouth
Reese's Peanut Butter Cup for garnish

Rim a martini glass with chocolate fudge. Shake ingredients with ice, and strain into the glass. Garnish with the Reese's Peanut Butter Cup.

 JILLY'S BISTRO • CHICAGO, IL

Alternative Martini

2 oz. Absolut Citron vodka
½ oz. Grand Marnier
Lemon twist for garnish

Shake with ice, and strain into a martini glass. Garnish with the lemon twist.

 JAMES ALLISON, JR. • BOISE, ID

Ambassador Martini

2 oz. Smirnoff vodka
Dash melon liqueur
Dash orange juice
Orange wheel for garnish

Shake with ice, and strain into a glass. Garnish
with the orange wheel.

Amber Dream Martini

2 parts Bombay Sapphire gin
1 part Martini & Rossi vermouth
3 dashes Chartreuse
Dash orange bitters

Shake with ice, and strain into a glass.

Amber Martini

1 oz. Sobieski vodka
½ oz. amaretto
½ oz. Frangelico

Shake with ice, and strain into a chilled martini
glass.

American Pie Martini

2 oz. Skyy vodka
¼ oz. Calvados
¼ oz. Stolichnaya Zinamon
Apple slice for garnish
Pinch cinnamon

Shake with ice, and strain into a martini glass.
Dip a side of the apple slice in cinnamon. Cut a
small slice into the apple so that it fits onto the
rim of the glass.

Americano

2 parts Martini & Rossi Rosso sweet vermouth
1 part Campari
Club soda to fill

Pour the first two ingredients over ice and stir.
Strain into a tall glass, and top with club soda.

Amethyst Martini

2 oz. Ketel One vodka
½ oz. Campari
½ oz. Chambord
Splash lime juice

Amides Martini

2 oz. Stolichnaya vodka
½ oz. Godiva original liqueur
Splash Frangelico
Almond or hazelnut for garnish

Shake with ice, and strain into a glass. Garnish with the almond or hazelnut.

Angel Martini

1 ½ oz. Ketel One vodka
½ oz. Frangelico

Shake with ice, and strain into a chilled martini glass.

Angelina Classy Lady

2 oz. Bacardi Limón rum
½ oz. 7-Up or Sprite
⅛ oz. Martini & Rossi extra dry vermouth
⅛ oz. Rose's Lime Juice

Annawanna/Tropical Martini

1 oz. Malibu coconut rum
½ oz. pineapple juice
Splash Rose's Lime Juice
Dash salt
Fruit of your choice for garnish

Shake, add ice, shake again, and strain into a chilled martini glass. Garnish with the fruit.

Annie's Raspberry Tartino

1 ½ oz. Stolichnaya Razberi vodka
½ oz. Chambord
Splash 7-Up
Splash fresh raspberry purée
Splash lemon juice

Shake with ice, and strain into a chilled martini glass.

 ANNIE PERONI • ANNIE'S CAFÉ • HARRISON, NY

Antini Martini

2 oz. Stolichnaya vodka
½ oz. Lillet Rouge
Burnt orange twist for garnish

Shake with ice, and strain into a chilled martini glass. Garnish with the ice-burnt orange twist.

 HARRY DENTON'S STARLIGHT ROOM
• SAN FRANCISCO, CA

Apple Jack Martini

Cinnamon sugar to rim
2 oz. Laird's Applejack brandy
Ground cinnamon
½ oz. Ketel One vodka

Rim the glass with cinnamon sugar. Muddle applejack brandy and cinnamon. Shake with vodka, and pour into the glass.

Apple Kiss Martini

Lime green sugar to rim
¾ oz. DeKuyper Sour Apple Pucker
  schnapps
¾ oz. vodka
½ scoop ice
Splash sour mix
Apple wedge for garnish

Rim a chilled martini glass with lime green sugar. Blend and serve frozen in the glass. Garnish with the apple wedge.

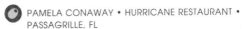 PAMELA CONAWAY • HURRICANE RESTAURANT • PASSAGRILLE, FL

Apple Martini

1 ½ oz. Glacier vodka
½ oz. Schoenauer Apfel schnapps
Dash cinnamon
Apple slice for garnish

Apple of My Eye

1 oz. Rain vodka
¾ oz. apple brandy
¼ oz. grenadine
¼ oz. lime juice

Shake with ice, and strain into a martini glass.
Serve straight up.

Appletini

2 oz. DeKuyper Sour Apple Pucker
   schnapps
1 ½ oz. Ketel One vodka
Apple slice for garnish

Shake with ice, and strain into a chilled martini
glass. Garnish with the slice of apple.

 BOBBY MCGEE'S • SAN BERNARDINO, CA

Appletini II

3 parts Bombay Sapphire gin
1 part Midori melon liqueur
Splash pineapple juice
Splash sweet and sour mix
Apple, cut into chunks
Apple slice for garnish

Shake hard with ice, and strain into a glass.
Garnish with the apple slice.

 MIKE SIMPSON • Il FORNAIO • SAN DIEGO, CA

Apres-Skitini

2 oz. Stolichnaya Zinamon
Splash mulled cider
Cinnamon stick for garnish

Serve in a warm martini glass, and garnish with
the cinnamon stick.

Apricot Martini

1 part Absolut vodka
1 part apricot brandy
1 part Godiva original liqueur
Maraschino cherry for garnish

Shake with ice, and strain into a glass. Serve
chilled. Garnish with the maraschino cherry.

Apry Amour

2 ½ oz. Sobieski vodka
½ oz. Marie Brizard Apry
Rose petal for garnish

Shake with ice, and strain into a martini glass.
Garnish with the rose petal.

Aquaman Martini

1 oz. aquavit
1 oz. Tanqueray gin
Dash dry vermouth
Olive for garnish

Shake with ice, and strain into a glass. Garnish
with the olive.

Aquarelle Martini

2 oz. Bacardi Limón rum
1 oz. Ketel One vodka
½ oz. Prunella Sauvage (local product)
2 drops blue curaçao
Lemon twist

 JOHN HYDE, BARTENDER • THE WATERGATE HOTEL
• WASHINGTON, DC

Aristicratico

2 ½ oz. Cuervo 1800 tequila
¼ oz. Grand Marnier
Jalapeño pepper for garnish

Shake with ice, and strain into a chilled martini
glass. Serve straight up or on the rocks. Garnish
with the jalapeño pepper.

Arlenie Martini

2 oz. limoncello
1 oz. Bombay Sapphire gin
1 oz. Frangelico
Dash rum

Shake with ice, and strain into a 4-oz. martini glass.

 STEVE VISAKAY • VINTAGE COCKTAIL SHAKERS

Army Cocktail Martini

2 oz. Bombay Sapphire gin
½ oz. sweet vermouth
Orange peel for garnish

Artillery Martini

2 oz. Tanqueray gin
1 oz. sweet vermouth

Shake with ice, and strain into a chilled glass.

Astoria Martini

1 ½ oz. Tanqueray dry gin
¾ oz. dry vermouth
Dash orange bitters
Green olive for garnish

Atta Boy Martini

2 oz. Tanqueray dry gin
½ oz. dry vermouth
2 dashes grenadine

Attitude-Tini

Sugar to rim
2 oz. Absolut Citron vodka
¼ oz. Cointreau
¼ oz. fresh lemon juice

Rim the glass with sugar. Shake with ice, and
strain into the glass.

 THE DINER ON SYCAMORE • CINCINNATI, OH

Atty Martini

2 oz. Tanqueray dry gin
½ oz. Martini & Rossi extra dry vermouth
2 dashes crème de violette
Lemon twist for garnish

B.V.D. Martini

¾ oz. Bacardi rum
¾ oz. Dubonnet Blanc
¾ oz. Martini & Rossi extra dry vermouth

Shake with ice, and strain into a chilled glass.

Babe Ruth Martini

¾ oz. butterscotch schnapps
¾ oz. dark crème de cacao
½ oz. Absolut vodka
Miniature Baby Ruth for garnish

Stir with ice, and strain into a chilled glass. Garnish with the miniature Baby Ruth.

 CHRIS "BARMAN" DAVIS • LODGE AT LAKEVIEW • AUSTIN, TX

Bacardi Dry Martini

2 oz. Bacardi rum
½ oz. Martini & Rossi extra dry vermouth

Shake with ice, and strain into a glass.

Bacardi Limón Martini

2 oz. Bacardi Limón rum
¾ oz. Martini & Rossi extra dry vermouth
Splash cranberry juice
Lemon twist for garnish

Shake with ice, and strain into a chilled martini glass. Garnish with the lemon twist.

Bacardi Seven Tiki Caribbean Martini

2 ½ oz. Bacardi Seven Tiki rum
½ oz. crème de bananes
Pineapple wedge or cube for garnish

Shake, and strain over ice. Serve straight up, and garnish with the pineapple wedge or cube.

Bacardi Sweet Martini

2 oz. Bacardi rum
2 oz. Martini & Rossi Rosso sweet vermouth

Shake with ice. Strain into chilled a martini glass.

Bad Apple Martini

1 ½ oz. Absolut Citron vodka
½ oz. Berentzen Apfel liqueur
2 drops Tabasco sauce
Apple slice for garnish

Shake vodka with ice, and strain into a chilled martini glass. Pour Berentzen down the side of the glass. Pour 2 drops of Tabasco into the center. Garnish with the apple slice.

 THE COUNTRY BARREL INN • CROSSWICKS, NJ

Baileys Chocolate Martini

1 ½ parts Baileys Irish cream
1 part Stolichnaya vodka
½ part crème de cacao
Maraschino cherry for garnish

Ballantine's Cocktail

1 ½ oz. Tanqueray dry gin
¾ oz. French vermouth
Dash orange bitters
Dash Pernod

Ballet Russe

2 oz. Stolichnaya vodka
¼ oz. Chambord
¼ oz. sour mix

 THE DINER ON SYCAMORE • CINCINNATI, OH

A Bally Good Martini

2 oz. Bombay Sapphire gin
⅛ oz. dry vermouth
⅛ oz. Grand Marnier
Orange twist for garnish

 BALLY'S • LAS VEGAS, NV

Bambou's Limón Martini

2 oz. Bacardi Limón rum
1 oz. Midori melon liqueur
½ oz. Martini & Rossi extra dry vermouth
Lemon twist for garnish

 REEBOK SPORTS CLUB • NEW YORK, NY

Banana Cream Pie Martini

1 part Cruzan rum cream
¼ part Cruzan banana rum

Shake with ice, and strain into a martini glass.

Banana Martini

2 ½ oz. Gordon's vodka
¼ oz. crème de bananes
Splash extra dry vermouth
Caramelized banana for garnish

Banzai Martini

2 ¾ oz. Skyy vodka
¼ oz. sake
⅛ oz. Martini & Rossi extra dry vermouth
Japanese pickled plum and shiso for garnish

Rinse glass with Martini & Rossi extra dry vermouth. Garnish with the Japanese pickled plum and shiso.

 BETELNUT • SAN FRANCISCO, CA

Barbarella

2 oz. vodka
Splash Martini & Rossi extra dry vermouth
Gorgonzola-stuffed olives for garnish

 WOLFGANG PUCK EXPRESS • WALT DISNEY
WORLD RESORT, FL

Barbed Wire

2 ½ oz. vodka
¼ oz. Martini & Rossi Rosso sweet vermouth
Splash Chambord
Splash Pernod
Maraschino cherry for garnish

 HARRIS' SAN FRANCISCO STEAKHOUSE • SAN
FRANCISCO, CA

Barnum Martini

1 ½ oz. Tanqueray gin
½ oz. DeKuyper Apricot brandy
4 dashes Angostura bitters
¼ tsp. fresh lemon juice

Shake with ice, and strain into a chilled glass.

Baron Martini

1 ½ oz. Tanqueray dry gin
½ oz. Martini & Rossi vermouth
¼ oz. orange curaçao
¼ oz. sweet vermouth
Lemon twist for garnish

Barry Martini

1 ½ oz. Bombay dry gin
¾ oz. Martini & Rossi Rosso sweet vermouth
Dash Angostura bitters
Dash white crème de menthe
Lemon twist for garnish

Stir the first three ingredients into a glass. Float crème de menthe on top. Garnish with the lemon twist.

Beauty Spot Martini

Dash grenadine
1 oz. Bombay Sapphire gin
½ oz. Martini & Rossi extra dry vermouth
½ oz. Martini & Rossi Rosso sweet vermouth
1 tsp. fresh orange juice

Put grenadine in the bottom of a chilled glass.
Shake the remaining ingredients with ice. Strain
into the glass, and don't stir.

Becco's Martini

1 ½ oz. Campari
1 ½ oz. Stolichnaya Ohranj vodka
½ oz. Martini & Rossi Rosso sweet vermouth
Orange peel for garnish

 REEBOK SPORTS CLUB • NEW YORK, NY

Beefeater Gin Rummy

1 part Beefeater dry gin
½ part Martini & Rossi vermouth
Dash bitters
Dash lemon juice

Shake with ice, and strain into a martini glass.

Bekah's Peanut Butter Cup

1 ½ oz. Frangelico
½ oz. Baileys Irish cream
½ oz. DeKuyper Buttershots schnapps
½ oz. Godiva original liqueur

Shake with ice, and strain into a frosted martini glass.

 MATT LESTER • JT'S SPORTS BAR/CLUB 22
• GRANGER, IN

Bel-Air Martini

2 oz. vodka
½ oz. sherry
Lemon twist for garnish

Bellini Martini

2 ½ oz. Stolichnaya vodka
½ oz. fresh white peach puree
Lemon zest for garnish

Shake with ice, and strain into a glass. Serve straight up or on the rocks. Garnish with the lemon zest.

 MARTINI'S • NEW YORK, NY

Belvedere Strawberry Mint Martini

2 fresh strawberries (plus 1 for garnish)
4 mint leaves (plus 1 for garnish)
2 oz. Belvedere vodka
½ oz. fresh lemon juice
½ oz. simple syrup

Muddle strawberries and mint with lemon juice and simple syrup. Add Belvedere, shake with ice, and strain into a chilled martini glass. Garnish with the strawberry and mint leaf.

 KATIE STEVENS • LAFORCE+STEVENS

Bennett Cocktail Martini

1 ½ oz. Tanqueray gin
⅓ oz. fresh lime juice
1 tsp. confectioners' sugar
2 dashes Angostura or orange bitters

Shake with ice, and strain into a chilled glass.

A Bentley Martini

2 oz. Calvados
1 oz. sweet vermouth
Lemon zest twist for garnish

Shake or stir with ice, and strain into a chilled glass. Serve straight up. Garnish with the lemon zest twist.

 TIM WORSTALL • SAN LUIS OBISPO, CA

Beri-Beri Nice

1 part Stolichnaya Razberi vodka
1 part Stolichnaya Strasberi vodka
Splash Chambord
Fresh raspberry for garnish

 PEGGY HOWELL • COTATI YACHT CLUB & SALOON • COTATI, CA

Bermuda Highball Martini

1 oz. Bombay Sapphire gin
1 oz. Martini & Rossi extra dry vermouth
1 oz. brandy
Cold club soda or ginger ale to fill
Lemon twist for garnish

Put two to three ice cubes in a chilled glass. Add gin, vermouth, and brandy. Top with club soda or ginger ale, stirring gently. Garnish with the lemon twist.

Bermudiana Rose

2 oz. Cork dry gin
¼ oz. apricot brandy
¼ oz. grenadine
¼ oz. lemon juice

Shake with ice, and strain into a glass.

Berry Berry Martini

2 oz. Beefeater gin
½ oz. cranberry cocktail
Fresh berry of your choice for garnish

Shake with ice, and strain into a chilled martini glass. Garnish with the fresh berry.

Berry Mocha Martini

1 ½ oz. Stolichnaya Razberi vodka
¼ oz. Godiva original liqueur
¼ oz. Kahlúa
Raspberries or chocolate for garnish

 KEELY KURTAS • ALLENTOWN BARTENDER
SCHOOL • WHITEHALL, PA

Big Apple Martini

3 oz. Finlandia vodka
1 ½ oz. sweet and sour mix
½ oz. DeKuyper Green Apple schnapps
Paper-thin wafer green apple for garnish

 BUBBLE LOUNGE • SAN FRANCISCO, CA

Bijou Cocktail Martini

1 oz. Bombay Sapphire gin
1 oz. green Chartreuse
1 oz. Martini & Rossi Rosso sweet vermouth
Dash orange bitters
Maraschino cherry for garnish

Stir with ice, and strain into a chilled glass.
Garnish with the maraschino cherry.

Bikini Martini

⅓ Absolut Citron vodka
⅓ Malibu rum
⅓ pineapple juice
Pineapple flag for garnish

 KEY CLUB HOLLYWOOD • HOLLYWOOD, CA

Bitch on Wheels

2 oz. Bombay Sapphire gin
¼ oz. Martini & Rossi extra dry vermouth
¼ oz. Pernod
¼ oz. white crème de menthe

Shake with ice, and strain into a chilled martini glass.

 STARS • SAN FRANCISCO, CA

Bitchin' Martini

1 ½ oz. Bombay Sapphire gin
½ oz. Martini & Rossi extra dry vermouth
1-2 dashes DeKuyper crème de menthe
1-2 dashes Pernod
Lemon twist for garnish

Stir with ice, and strain into a glass. Garnish with the lemon twist.

Bittersweet Martini

1 ½ oz. Martini & Rossi extra dry vermouth
1 ½ oz. Martini & Rossi Rosso sweet vermouth
Dash Angostura bitters
Dash orange bitters
Orange twist for garnish

Shake with ice, and strain into a chilled glass.
Garnish with the orange twist.

Black Currant Martini

1 oz. Godiva original liqueur
1 oz. Seagram's gin
¼ oz. crème de cassis
¼ oz. lemon juice
¼ oz. lime juice
Maraschino cherry for garnish

Shake with ice, and strain into a cocktail glass.
Garnish with the maraschino cherry.

Black Eyed "P"

3 oz. Absolut Peppar vodka
Black olives for garnish

Shake with ice, and strain into a chilled martini
glass. Serve on the rocks or straight up. Garnish
with the olives.

 CECILIA'S • BRECKENRIDGE, CO

Black Jack Daniel's

Sugar to rim
2 ½ oz. Jack Daniel's
¼ oz. fresh lemon juice

Rim a chilled martini glass with sugar. Shake
with ice, and strain into the glass. Serve straight
up or on the rocks.

 THE DINER ON SYCAMORE • CINCINNATI, OH

Black Jack Martini

2 oz. Jack Daniel's
¼ oz. sweet vermouth
Dash Angostura bitters
Maraschino for garnish

Shake with ice, and strain into a chilled martini glass. Garnish with the maraschino cherry.

 HERBERT KERSCHBAUMER • JACK'S RESTAURANT & BAR • WASHINGTON, DC

Black Magic

1 ½ oz. Jägermeister
1 ½ oz. vodka

Chill, and serve straight up.

Black Martini

1 ½ oz. Absolut Kurant vodka
Splash Chambord

Stir ingredients with ice, and strain into a glass. Serve straight up or on the rocks.

 CONTINENTAL CAFÉ • PHILADELPHIA, PA

Black Stallion Martini

2 oz. Smirnoff vodka
Dash Romana Black sambuca
3 espresso beans for garnish

Shake with ice, and strain into a glass. Garnish with the three espresso beans.

Black Tie Martini

1 ½ oz. Skyy vodka
Spritz Campari
Spritz Chivas Regal
2 cocktail onions for garnish
1 black olive for garnish

Blackberry Martini

1 ½ oz. Chambord
1 ½ oz. Stolichnaya Vanil

Shake with ice, and strain into a chilled martini glass. Serve straight up or on the rocks.

Bleeding Heart Martini

Splash Campari
6 oz. Ketel One vodka
Black olive for garnish

Chill a bottle of Campari in freezer until it gets syrupy. Wet and chill a cocktail glass in the freezer as well. Swirl the vodka with ice, and strain into the cocktail glass. Slowly pour the Campari around the rim of the glass. Garnish with the black olive.

 THOMAS ROZYCKI • BLOOMSBURG, PA

Blenton Martini

1 ½ oz. Tanqueray dry gin
¾ oz. Martini & Rossi extra dry vermouth
Dash Angostura bitters
Lemon twist for garnish

Bleu Martini

2 ½ oz. Frïs vodka
¼ oz. dry vermouth
Olives stuffed with bleu cheese for garnish

Shake with ice, and strain into the martini glass. Serve on the rocks or in a chilled glass. Garnish with the olives.

Blimlet Martini

2 oz. Martini & Rossi extra dry vermouth
2 oz. Rose's Lime Juice
1 oz. lemon juice
½ oz. crème de cassis

Blonde Martini

2 ½ oz. Bombay Sapphire gin
¼ oz. Lillet Blonde

Shake with ice, and strain into a martini glass.
Serve straight up or on the rocks in a chilled glass.

 BRASSERIE JO • CHICAGO, IL

Blood and Sand Martini

¾ oz. cherry brandy
¾ oz. Dewar's Blended scotch whiskey
¾ oz. fresh orange juice
¾ oz. Martini & Rossi Rosso sweet vermouth

Shake with ice, and strain into a chilled glass.

Blood Ohranj Martini

3 parts Stolichnaya Ohranj vodka
1 part Campari
Splash club soda

Stir with ice, and strain into a glass.

Bloodhound Martini

1 oz. gin
½ oz. Fragoli
½ oz. Martini & Rossi extra dry vermouth
½ oz. Martini & Rossi Rosso sweet vermouth
Strawberry for garnish

Shake with ice, and strain into a chilled glass.
Garnish with the strawberry.

Bloody Martini

2 oz. Smirnoff vodka
Dash tomato juice
Generous shake Tabasco sauce
Generous shake Worcestershire sauce
Freshly grated horseradish to top
Lime wedge for garnish

Shake with ice, and strain into a martini glass.
Top with horseradish, and garnish with the lime.

Bloody Orange Martini

2 oz. 4 Orange vodka
¼ oz. Campari

Shake with ice, and strain into a chilled martini glass.

Blue Dolphin Martini

2 oz. Finlandia vodka, chilled
1 oz. grapefruit juice
¼ oz. blue curaçao
¼ oz. Grand Marnier
2 drops Rose's Lime Juice

Shake with ice, and strain into a chilled martini glass. Serve on the rocks or straight up.

Blue Gordon's Martini

2 ½ oz. Gordon's vodka
¼ oz. blue curaçao
Lemon twist for garnish

Shake with ice, and strain into a martini glass. Serve straight up or on the rocks in a chilled glass. Garnish with the lemon twist.

Blue Lagoon Martini

1 ¼ oz. Bacardi Limón rum
½ oz. blue curaçao
¼ oz. dry vermouth
Strawberry or olives for garnish

 ALEX REFOJO • CLUB MYSTIQUE • MIAMI, FL

Blue Martini

1 oz. Stolichnaya Citros vodka
1 oz. Stolichnaya Razberi vodka
Splash sour mix
Dash curaçao
Lemon twist for garnish

Blue Monday Martini

1 ½ oz. Smirnoff vodka
¾ oz. triple sec
Dash blue curaçao
Orange slice for garnish

Shake with ice, and strain into a glass. Garnish
with the orange slice.

Blue Period Martini

1 ½ oz. Absolut vodka
½ oz. Leyden gin
¼ oz. blue curaçao
¼ oz. pineapple juice
¼ oz. Sprite

Shake with ice, except for the Sprite. Strain into a chilled martini glass. Serve straight up or on the rocks.

 MARTINI CLUB • ATLANTA, GA

Blue Room Martini

3 oz. Stolichnaya Peachik vodka
Splash blue curaçao
Splash sour mix
Twist for garnish

Shake with ice, and strain into a glass. Garnish with the twist.

Blue Sapphire Martini

3 oz. Bombay Sapphire gin
1 oz. blue curaçao
Splash dry vermouth
Maraschino cherry for garnish

Stir with ice, and strain into a chilled martini glass. Garnish with the maraschino cherry.

 THE MANDARIN ORIENTAL • SAN FRANCISCO, CA

Blue Shark Martini

1 ½ oz. tequila
1 ½ oz. vodka
½ oz. blue curaçao

Shake with ice, and strain into a chilled martini glass. Serve straight up or on the rocks.

Blue Skyy Martini

2 ½ oz. Skyy vodka
Splash blue curaçao

Stir with ice, and strain into a chilled martini glass.

 COMPASS ROSE • SAN FRANCISCO, CA

Blue Water

2 oz. Skyy vodka
¼ oz. blue curaçao

Shake with ice, and strain into a glass. Serve straight up or on the rocks.

 SABA BLUE WATER CAFÉ • AUSTIN, TX

Blue-Doo Child Martini

2 oz. pineapple juice
2 oz. Stolichnaya Blueberi vodka
½ oz. DeKuyper Tropical Mango liqueur
¼ oz. blue curaçao
Pineapple slice for garnish

Shake the first three ingredients with ice. Strain into a martini glass, and drizzle in blue curaçao. It will sink to the bottom. Garnish with the pineapple slice.

 FRANK RYAN • SENECA NIAGARA CASINO & HOTEL • NIAGARA FALLS, NY

Blue-Eyed Tomcat

2 ½ oz. Bombay Sapphire gin
Tomolives for garnish

Shake with ice, and strain into a chilled martini
glass. Serve straight up or on the rocks. Garnish
with the Tomolives.

 CECILIA'S • BRECKENRIDGE, CO

Blues Martini

½ oz. Bombay Sapphire gin
½ oz. Ketel One vodka
Few drops blue curaçao

Stir gently with ice, and strain into a glass. Serve
straight up or on the rocks.

Bobby Burns Martini

1 ½ oz. Martini & Rossi Rosso sweet vermouth
1 ½ oz. scotch
¼ oz. Benedictine
Lemon twist for garnish

Stir, and strain into a chilled glass. Garnish with
the lemon twist.

Bombay Martini

3 oz. Bombay Sapphire gin
Splash Martini & Rossi extra dry vermouth
Bleu cheese–stuffed olive for garnish

 GIBSON'S • CHICAGO, IL

Bonnie Prince Martini

1 ½ oz. dry gin
½ oz. Lillet
¼ oz. Drambuie

Shake with ice, and strain into a chilled martini
glass. Serve on the rocks or straight up.

Bookmark

2 oz. Ketel One vodka
½ oz. Chambord
Tomolive for garnish

Shake with ice, and strain into a chilled martini
glass. Serve straight up or on the rocks. Garnish
with the Tomolive.

Boomerang Martini

4 parts dry gin
1 part Martini & Rossi extra dry vermouth
1 part Martini & Rossi Rosso sweet vermouth
2 dashes maraschino cherry juice
Lemon twist for garnish

Bootlegger Martini

1 ½ oz. Bombay Sapphire gin
½ oz. Southern Comfort
Lemon twist for garnish

Shake with ice, and strain into a chilled martini glass. Serve straight up or on the rocks.

 CHIANTI • HOUSTON, TX

Boru Martini

2 ½ oz. Boru Original vodka
¼ oz. Boru Orange or Citrus vodka
Orange or lemon peel for garnish

Shake gently with ice, and strain into a chilled martini glass. Garnish with the orange or lemon peel.

Boston Bullet Martini

2 oz. dry gin
½ oz. dry vermouth
Almond-stuffed green olive for garnish

Boticelli Martini

1 ¼ oz. Bombay Sapphire gin
1 ¼ oz. Ketel One vodka
Goat cheese–stuffed olive for garnish

 KEVIN JASON • RESTORANTE PRIMAVERA •
MILLIS, MA

Bowery

1 part Campari
1 part Godiva original liqueur
1 part Ketel One vodka

Stir, strain into a martini glass, and serve.

Boxer Martini

2 oz. Absolut vodka
1 oz. Absolut Peppar vodka
½ oz. Dubonnet Blanc (or vermouth)

Brandied Madeira Martini

1 oz. brandy
1 oz. Madeira
½ oz. dry vermouth
Lemon twist for garnish

Stir with ice, and strain into a chilled glass over ice cubes. Garnish with the lemon twist.

Brave Cow Martini

1 ½ oz. Bombay Sapphire gin
½ oz. coffee liqueur

Shake with ice, and strain into a chilled martini glass.

Brazil Cocktail Martini

1 ½ oz. dry sherry
1 ½ oz. dry vermouth
Dash Angostura bitters
Dash Pernod or other anise-flavored
   liqueur
Lemon twist for garnish

Stir with ice, and strain into a chilled glass. Garnish with the lemon twist.

Breakfast Martini

2 oz. Stolichnaya Ohranj
½ oz. orange marmalade
Orange zest for garnish

Shake with ice, and strain into a martini glass.
Garnish with the orange zest.

 LOT 61 • NEW YORK, NY

Brit Martini

2 oz. Beefeater gin
½ oz. Pimm's No. 1 Cup
Cucumber slice for garnish

Shake with ice, and strain into a chilled martini
glass. Serve straight up or on the rocks.

 POLO LOUNGE • WINDSOR COURT HOTEL •
NEW ORLEANS, LA

Bronx Golden

2 oz. Beefeater gin
⅛ oz. dry vermouth
⅛ oz. orange juice
⅛ oz. sweet vermouth
1 egg yolk

Shake with ice for 15 seconds, and strain into a chilled martini glass.

Bronx Martini

2 oz. Beefeater gin
¼ oz. Martini & Rossi extra dry vermouth
¼ oz. Martini & Rossi Rosso sweet vermouth
¼ oz. orange juice
Lemon twist for garnish

Shake with ice, and strain into a chilled martini glass. Serve straight up or on the rocks.

 MR. BABBINGTON'S • NEW YORK, NY

Bronx Terrace Cocktail

1 ½ oz. gin
¾ oz. fresh lime juice
½ oz. dry vermouth
Maraschino cherry for garnish

Shake with ice, and strain into a chilled glass.
Garnish with the maraschino cherry.

Brown Cocktail Martini

1 oz. gin
1 oz. light rum
¾ oz. dry vermouth

Stir ingredients with ice, and strain into a
chilled glass.

Buckeye Martini

2 oz. Smirnoff vodka
½ oz. dry vermouth
Black olive for garnish

Shake with ice, and strain into a glass. Garnish
with the black olive.

Buff Martini

2 oz. Finlandia vodka
½ oz. Baileys Irish cream
½ oz. Kahlúa
Sprinkle of freshly ground coffee or cinnamon for garnish

Stir gently with ice, and strain into a glass. Garnish with the sprinkle of freshly ground coffee or cinnamon.

Bulldog

1 ½ oz. Beefeater gin
1 ½ oz. orange juice
Ginger ale to fill
Maraschino cherry or orange twist for garnish

Stir juice and gin over ice in a Collins glass. Fill with ginger ale. Garnish with the maraschino cherry or orange twist.

Bunny Hug Martini

1 oz. dry gin
1 oz. Pernod
1 oz. whiskey

Shake with ice, and strain into a glass.

Burnt Martini

1 ½ oz. Beefeater gin
Splash scotch
Lemon twist for garnish

Shake with ice, and strain into a glass. Garnish
with the lemon twist.

 ANITA SHOLDICE • QUALICUM BEACH, BC

Cabaret Cocktail

2 oz. dry gin
¼ oz. Benedictine
¼ oz. dry vermouth
2 dashes Angostura bitters
Maraschino cherry for garnish

Cajun King Martini

1 ½ oz. Absolut Peppar vodka
½ oz. Absolut Citron vodka
1-2 dashes dry vermouth
Small jalapeño peppers for garnish

Cajun Martini

2 ½ oz. Absolut Peppar vodka
¼ oz. dry vermouth
Tomolives for garnish

Shake with ice, and strain into a chilled martini glass. Serve straight up or on the rocks. Garnish with the Tomolives.

Calypso Splash

2 oz. dry gin
¼ oz. blue curaçao
¼ oz. pineapple juice

Shake with ice, and strain into a chilled martini glass. Serve straight up or on the rocks.

 RED LOBSTER • MEMPHIS, TN

Campari Margie

2 oz. Campari
2 oz. sour mix
½ oz. Cointreau
Dash Rose's Lime Juice

Shake with ice, and strain into a chilled martini glass.

Campari Passion

1 ½ oz. Skyy Infusions Passion Fruit vodka
¾ oz. Campari
¾ oz. mango juice
¾ oz. orange juice
½ oz. freshly squeezed lemon juice
Lemon zest for garnish

Pour ingredients in a mixing pint over ice.
Shake vigorously, and strain into a martini glass.
Garnish with the lemon zest.

Campari Viceroy

2 oz. Campari
½ oz. Disaronno amaretto
½ oz. Southern Comfort
⅛ oz. orange juice
⅛ oz. pineapple juice

Shake with ice, and strain into a highball glass
over ice.

Campartini

2 oz. Campari
2 oz. Stolichnaya Ohranj vodka
Dash Rose's Lime Juice
Splash orange juice
Orange slice for garnish

Shake with ice, and strain into a chilled martini glass. Garnish with the orange slice.

Campton Cosmo Martini

1 ½ oz. Absolut Citron vodka
½ oz. lemon juice
¼ oz. Tuaca
Splash cranberry juice
1 kumquat for garnish

Stir with ice, and strain into a chilled martini glass. Garnish with the kumquat.

Campton Cure Martini

1 oz. Absolut Citron vodka
½ oz. Cointreau
3 squeezes lime juice
Splash cranberry juice

Stir with ice, and strain into a chilled martini glass.

 CAMPTON PLACE HOTEL • SAN FRANCISCO, CA

Canadian Cocktail

1 ½ oz. Canadian Club Classic 12
½ tsp. sugar
½ oz. DeKuyper triple sec
Dash bitters

Shake with ice, and strain into a chilled martini glass.

Candy-Cane Martini

Sugar to rim glass
2 ½ oz. Sobieski vodka
¼ oz. green crème de menthe

Rim the glass with sugar. Shake with ice, and strain into the glass.

Cane Juice

Cinnamon sugar to rim
1 ½ oz. 10 Cane rum
1 ½ oz. fresh lemon sour
1 oz. chai syrup
1 ½ tbs. apricot preserves
Splash Grand Marnier
Dried apricot for garnish

Rim the glass with cinnamon sugar. Combine rum, lemon sour, chai syrup, and apricot preserves. Shake vigorously with ice, and strain into the glass. Float a splash of Grand Marnier on top. Garnish with the dried apricot.

 BOA STEAKHOUSE • THE FORUM SHOPS AT CAESARS • LAS VEGAS, NV

Canton Martini

2 oz. Grey Goose
½ oz. Domaine de Canton French Ginger liqueur
½ oz. Grand Marnier
Candied ginger slice for garnish

Shake vigorously with ice, and strain into a glass. Garnish with the candied ginger slice.

 BRAD NELSON • 56 WEST • CHICAGO, IL

Capital "G" Martini

2 oz. Gordon's vodka
⅛ oz. vermouth
Tomolive for garnish

Shake with ice, and strain into a chilled martini glass. Serve straight up or on the rocks. Garnish with the Tomolive.

Capoutini

2 oz. Leyden dry gin
Splash raspberry puree
3 or 4 raspberries for garnish

 JACQUES CAPSOUTO • CAPSOUTO RESTAURANT •
NEW YORK, NY

Caprice Martini

1 ½ oz. dry gin
½ oz. Benedictine
½ oz. dry vermouth
Dash orange bitters

Cardamom Martini

8-9 cardamom seeds (plus 3 more for
  garnish)
2 ½ oz. Belvedere vodka
½ oz. sugar syrup

Muddle eight to nine cardamom seeds with vodka
and sugar syrup. Shake well, and strain into a martini glass. Garnish with three cardamom seeds.

Caribe Martini

1 oz. Bacardi rum
1 oz. Mount Gay rum
Dash pineapple juice

 NO. 18 • NEW YORK, NY

Caribbean Surfer

1 oz. Bacardi rum
1 oz. Captain Morgan Parrot Bay Coconut
  rum
½ oz. banana liqueur
½ oz. pineapple juice

Shake with ice, and strain into a chilled martini
glass.

 THE PARKER HOUSE • SEA GIRT, NJ

Carnival Martini

2 ½ oz. vodka
½ oz. orange juice
¼ oz. fresh lime juice

Shake with ice, and strain into a chilled martini glass. Serve straight up or on the rocks.

 COCONUT GROVE • SAN FRANCISCO, CA

Carroll Cocktail Martini

1 ½ oz. brandy
¾ oz. Martini & Rossi Rosso sweet vermouth
Maraschino cherry for garnish

Stir with ice, and strain into a chilled glass. Garnish with the maraschino cherry.

Cary Grant

Martini & Rossi extra dry vermouth to rinse
2 ½ oz. Luksusowa Original Potato vodka
    (Polish vodka)
½ oz. fresh lime juice
Splash Tio Pepe dry sherry

 BALBOA • SAN FRANCISCO, CA

Casino Cocktail

2 oz. Tanqueray gin
¼ oz. lemon juice
¼ oz. maraschino cherry juice
2 dashes Angostura bitters

Castries PB&J

2 oz. Castries Peanut Rum Crème
1 oz. premium vodka
1 tbsp. grape jelly

Shake together with ice, and strain into a martini glass or on the rocks.

 POLLY RYERSON • PR PR • NASHVILLE, TN

Catalina Martini

2 ½ oz. Gordon's vodka
½ oz. extra dry vermouth
½ oz. peach schnapps
Lemon twist soaked in Grand Marnier for
   garnish

Catherine the Great Martini

2 oz. Absolut vodka
½ oz. Cointreau
¼ oz. framboise
Champagne to fill

Shake the first three ingredients together, and strain into a champagne flute. Top with champagne.

Cecilia's Bold

1 oz. Absolut Peppar vodka
1 oz. Beefeater gin
¼ oz. Italian dry vermouth
Italian hot pepper for garnish

Shake with ice, and strain into a chilled martini glass. Serve straight up or on the rocks. Garnish with the hot pepper.

 CECILIA'S • BRECKENRIDGE, CO

Celebrity Martini

Rose's Lime Juice for rinsing
2 ½ oz. gin
1 oz. Alizé
½ oz. Grand Marnier
Lemon and lime twists for garnish

Rinse martini glass with Rose's lime juice. Shake remaining ingredients over ice, and strain into a glass. Garnish with the lemon and lime twists.

 CHRIS GOLZ • FORBIDDEN FRUIT •
LONG BEACH, CA

Celtic Continental

2 oz. Celtic Crossing liqueur
¼ oz. Chambord
¼ oz. peach schnapps

Shake with ice, and strain into a chilled martini glass.

Celtic Martini

1 part Celtic Crossing liqueur
1 part lemon vodka
Lemon twist for garnish

Champagne Martini

¼ oz. DeKuyper Vanilla Delight liquer
1 oz. Finlandia vodka
¼ oz. Chambord
1 oz. Korbel Brut champagne
Red rose petal for garnish

Chill a martini glass. Fill a spray bottle with DeKuyper Vanilla Delight. In a martini shaker add ice, Finlandia, and Chambord. Liberally fill inner surface of martini glass with the DeKuyper Vanilla Delight. Add the contents of the cocktail shaker, and fill the remainder of the glass with cold champagne. Garnish with the rose petal.

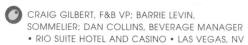 CRAIG GILBERT, F&B VP; BARRIE LEVIN, SOMMELIER; DAN COLLINS, BEVERAGE MANAGER
• RIO SUITE HOTEL AND CASINO • LAS VEGAS, NV

Champagne Royale de Martini

1 ½ oz. premium vodka
1 oz. Veuve Clicquot Yellow Label champagne
½ oz. Chambord raspberry liqueur
Lemon twist for garnish

Stir with ice, and strain into a chilled martini glass. Garnish with the lemon twist.

TONGUE & GROOVE • ATLANTA, GA

Chartrini Martini

2 ½ oz. vodka
¼ oz. Chartreuse

Shake with ice, and strain into a chilled martini glass. Serve straight up or on the rocks.

Chatterly Martini

2 oz. dry gin
½ oz. dry vermouth
¼ oz. orange curaçao

Cheap Thrill

Chocolate syrup to dress glass
DeKuyper Thrilla Vanilla
Splash vodka
Whipped cream for garnish
Cinnamon for garnish

Serve very cold with the glass lightly drizzled with chocolate syrup. Garnish drink with a touch of whipped cream and cinnamon.

Chekhov Coffee Martini

1 part Romana Black sambuca
1 part Stolichnaya Kafya vodka

Strain into a martini glass, and serve straight up.

Cherries Jubilee

Sugar to rim
2 oz. Skyy Infusions Cherry vodka
½ oz. Carolans Irish cream
½ oz. Cointreau
Maraschino cherry for garnish

Rim a martini glass with sugar. Shake with ice, and strain into the glass. Garnish with the cherry.

 J. DANIEL • SAN FRANCISCO, CA

Cherry Ripe Martini

1 ½ oz. Smirnoff vodka
½ oz. brandy
½ oz. cherry brandy
Maraschino cherry for garnish

Shake with ice, and strain into a glass. Garnish with the maraschino cherry.

Cherry Tree

2 ½ oz. Skyy vodka
¼ oz. cherry liqueur
Maraschino cherry for garnish

Shake with ice, and garnish with the maraschino cherry.

Chesapeake Martini

2 oz. Absolut Peppar vodka
1 tbsp. clam or oyster liquid
½ tsp. Old Bay seasoning
2 dashes hot sauce
1 cherry tomato
1 fresh oyster

 HARBOR COURT • BALTIMORE, MD

Chesterfield

1–2 drops Martini & Rossi extra dry vermouth
2 oz. Belvedere vodka
¼ oz. Cointreau
Pinch sugar
Juice ½ orange (plus ½ orange)
Juice ¼ lemon
¼ oz. sour mix
Twist for garnish

Place vermouth in an iced cup. Fill with ice. Add vodka. Add Cointreau and sugar. Add orange juice, the orange (including rind), and lemon juice. Add sour mix. Shake until cold, and strain into a chilled glass. Garnish with the twist. For sweet occasions, sugar the rim of the martini glass.

 LOLA'S • CHICAGO, IL

Chicago Lake Breeze Martini

1 ½ oz. Stolichnaya Peachik vodka
Splash 7-Up
Splash cranberry juice
Lemon twist for garnish

Shake with ice, and strain into a chilled martini glass. Serve on the rocks or straight up. Garnish with the lemon twist.

Chicago Martini

2 oz. Bombay dry gin
½ oz. Dewar's Blended scotch whiskey
Green olive for garnish

Shake with ice, and strain into a chilled martini glass. Serve on the rocks or straight up. Garnish with the green olive.

Chili Pepper Martini

1 ¼ oz. Skyy vodka
¼ oz. Goldschläger
⅛ oz. chili pepper

Shake well with ice, and strain into a chilled martini glass.

Chilly Willy

2 oz. Stolichnaya
½ oz. Rumple Minze schnapps

Shake with ice, and strain into a chilled martini glass.

China Blue Martini

2 ½ oz. gin
¼ oz. blue curaçao
¼ oz. Domaine de Canton French Ginger liqueur
Crystallized ginger for garnish

Shake with ice, and strain into a chilled martini glass. Serve straight up or on the rocks. Garnish with the ginger.

 THE MARTINI CLUB • ATLANTA, GA

Chinese Skyy Line Martini

Skyy vodka
Chilled sake to float

Shake with ice, and strain into an oversized martini glass. Serve straight up. Float sake.

Chinook Martini

2 oz. Smirnoff vodka
2 parts fresh raspberries
1 part fresh blueberries
Dash lime cordial

Infuse vodka with raspberries and blueberries. Add lime cordial. Shake with ice, and strain into a glass. Garnish with the fresh berries.

Chocatini

1 ¼ oz. Grey Goose vodka
½ oz. white crème de cacao

Shake with ice, and strain into a chilled martini
glass. Serve on the rocks or straight up.

 SID MAPLES • JULIE'S SUPPER CLUB • SAN
FRANCISCO, CA

Chocolate Choo Choo Martini

2 ½ oz. Absolut vodka
¼ oz. Godiva original liqueur
¼ oz. Kahlúa
Chocolate Kiss for garnish

Shake with ice, and strain into a chilled martini
glass. Serve straight up or on the rocks. Garnish
with the Chocolate Kiss.

Chocolate Ghost Martini

1 oz. Stolichnaya vodka
½ oz. white crème de cacao

Shake with ice, and strain into a chilled martini
glass.

 TOBY ELLIS • T.G.I. FRIDAY'S • CHEVY CHASE, MD

Chocolate Hazelnut

2 oz. Skyy vodka
½ oz. crème de cacao
½ oz. Frangelico

Shake with ice, and strain into a chilled martini glass. Serve straight up or on the rocks.

Chocolate Mint Martini

1 ¼ oz. Cruzan Estate light rum
¾ oz. dark crème de cacao
¼ oz. Cruzan rum cream
¼ oz. white crème de menthe

Shake the first three ingredients with ice, and strain into a martini glass. Top with white crème de menthe.

Chocolate Raspberry Martini

2 oz. Belvedere vodka
¼ oz. dark chocolate liqueur
¼ oz. white chocolate liqueur
⅛ oz. Martini & Rossi Rosso sweet vermouth
⅛ oz. raspberry liqueur
Raspberry marinated in vodka

Shake with ice, and strain into a chilled martini glass. Serve straight up or on the rocks. Garnish with the raspberry.

Chocolate Rose

1 oz. dark crème de cacao
1 oz. De Kuyper Razzmatazz
1 oz. Tequila Rose
Splash milk

Shake with ice, and strain into a martini glass.

 BITSY NELSON • LINDENWOLD MOOSE LODGE
#548 • LINDENWOLD, NJ

Chocolate-Covered Cherry Martini

1 ¾ oz. vodka
¼ oz. white crème de cacao
Splash Grand Marnier
Maraschino cherry for garnish

Shake with ice, and strain into a chilled martini glass. Garnish with the maraschino cherry.

Chocolate-Covered Raspberry

2 oz. Stolichnaya Razberi
1 oz. Godet Belgian white chocolate liqueur

Shake with ice, and strain into a chilled martini glass.

Chocolatini

1 ½ oz. Godiva original liqueur
1 oz. Stolichnaya Vanil vodka
Hershey's Kiss, chocolate dipped cherries,
   or a marshmallow for garnish

Shake with ice, and strain into a chilled martini
glass. Garnish with the Hershey's Kiss, chocolate
dipped cherries, or marshmallow.

Choco-Raspberry Martini

1 ½ oz. Stolichnaya Razberi vodka
½ oz. crème de cacao
½ oz. Stolichnaya Vanil vodka

Shake with ice, and strain into a chilled martini
glass.

Chocotini I

2 oz. Stolichnaya Ohranj vodka
¼ oz. Godiva original liqueur
Orange slice for garnish

Serve straight up or on the rocks. Garnish with
the orange slice.

 JILL STEVENS • TRABUCO CANYON, CA

Choicetini

3 oz. vodka
2 oz. champagne
1 oz. fresh pineapple juice
1 oz. white peach puree
Pineapple slice for garnish

Shake with ice, and strain into a chilled martini glass. Garnish with the pineapple slice.

 RACHELANN HARRISON • KITCHEN & COCKTAILS • NEW YORK, NY

Chopin's #8

1 ½ oz. Chopin vodka
¼ oz. Chambord
¼ oz. cranberry juice to float
Fresh raspberry for garnish

Shake vigorously with ice, and strain into a frozen cocktail glass. Float cranberry juice. Garnish with the raspberry, letting it sink to the bottom.

 JULIE GRANT • PUZZLES • ATLANTA, GA

Cinnamon and Spice

2 oz. Bacardi Seven Tiki rum
⅛ oz. Martini & Rossi Rosso sweet vermouth
Two cinnamon sticks for garnish

Shake with ice, and strain into a glass. Garnish with the cinnamon sticks.

 RED HEAD'S • CHICAGO, IL

Cinnamon Martini

2 ½ oz. Smirnoff vodka
Dash cinnamon schnapps
Cinnamon stick for garnish

Shake with ice, and strain into a glass. Garnish with the cinnamon stick.

Cinnamon Toast Martini

¼ oz. cinnamon schnapps
2 oz. Absolut vodka, frozen
1 cinnamon wafer

Line the glass with schnapps, and pour out excess. Pour in vodka. Stir with the wafer.

 JEREMY GORING • THE OBSERVATORY HOTEL • SYDNEY, AUSTRALIA

Cirocaccino

1 ½ oz. Cîroc vodka
1 oz. cold espresso
1 tsp. simple syrup
Baileys Irish cream, foamed, to top
Milk to top

Shake well with ice, and strain into a martini
glass. Top with Baileys Irish cream and milk.

 EDEN FREEMAN • NEW YORK, NY

Citron Martini

1 ¼ oz. Absolut Citron vodka
Dash Martini & Rossi extra dry vermouth
Twist or olive for garnish

Shake or stir well with ice. Strain into a cocktail
glass. Serve straight up or over ice. Garnish with
the twist or olive.

Citron Martini II

2 oz Absolut Citron vodka
½ oz. Chambord

Shake with ice, and strain into a chilled martini
glass. Serve straight up or on the rocks.

 PORTLAND'S BEST • PORTLAND, OR

Citronini

Sugar to rim
2 oz. Absolut Citron vodka
½ oz. lemon juice
½ oz. sour mix

Rim a martini glass with sugar. Shake with ice, and strain into a chilled martini glass. Serve straight up or on the rocks.

 HURRICANE RESTAURANT • PASSAGRILLE, FL

Citrus Martini

2 oz. Stolichnaya Citros vodka
¾ oz. Cointreau
¼ oz. lemon juice

 PRAVDA • NEW YORK, NY

Citrus-Tini

2 oz. Absolut Citron vodka
¼ oz. Grand Marnier
Dash Rose's Lime Juice
Lime or lemon twist for garnish

 BRIAN MISENHEIMER • HOULIHAN'S • GREENSBORO, NC

Claridge Martini

1 oz. Bombay Sapphire gin
1 oz. Martini & Rossi extra dry vermouth
½ oz. apricot brandy
½ oz. triple sec or Cointreau

Shake with ice, and strain into a chilled glass.

Classic Dry Martini

2 ½ oz. Bombay Sapphire gin
Splash vermouth
Lemon twist

 THE MARTINI CLUB • ATLANTA, GA

Classic Fintini

3 oz. Finlandia vodka, chilled
Garnish optional

Shake with ice, and strain into a chilled martini
glass. Serve straight up or on the rocks.

Classic Olive Martini

2 ½ oz. Ketel One vodka
1 drop dry vermouth
1 drop olive juice
3 Sicilian olives for garnish

Chill until bone-rattling cold. Strain into a glass.
Garnish with the olives.

 JEFF NACE • OLIVES • BOSTON, MA

Classic Vodka Martini

2 ½ oz. Stolichnaya vodka, chilled
Lemon twist for garnish

Shake with ice, and strain into a glass. Garnish
with the lemon twist.

 RENAISSANCE ATLANTA HOTEL • ATLANTA, GA

Cleanhead

1 ½ oz. Stolichnaya vodka
Tonic water to top
2 lime segments

Strain vodka over ice, and top with tonic.
Garnish with the lime segments. Squeeze
limes well.

Clementini

2 oz. Stolichnaya Ohranj vodka
½ oz. Grand Marnier
Fresh clementine sections

Shake with ice, and strain into a glass. Garnish with the clementine sections.

Cloudy Day Martini

2 ½ oz. Absolut vodka
¼ oz. Opal Nera
Espresso bean for garnish

Shake with ice, and strain into a chilled martini glass. Serve straight up or on the rocks. Garnish with the espresso bean.

Cloudy Skies Martini

2 ½ oz. Skyy vodka
¼ oz. sambuca
Lemon twist for garnish

Shake with ice, and strain into a chilled martini glass. Serve straight up or on the rocks. Garnish with the lemon twist.

 THE WINDSOCK BAR & GRILL • SAN DIEGO, CA

Clove Martini

3 ½ oz. Belvedere vodka
Freshly ground cloves

Shake with ice, and strain into a glass.

Club Cocktail Martini

1 ½ oz. Beefeater dry gin
¾ oz. Martini & Rossi Rosso sweet vermouth
¼ oz. yellow Chartreuse
Maraschino cherry or green olive for garnish

Club Lady's Famous In & Out Martini

"Always chill before you fill."

¼ oz. Martini & Rossi extra dry vermouth
2 ½ oz. Belvedere vodka
Bleu cheese–stuffed Spanish olives for
    garnish
Lemon twist for garnish

Chill a 4- to 6-oz. martini glass. Add vermouth
and discard, thus the name "In and Out." Shake
with vodka for about 30 seconds, and strain into
a martini glass. Garnish with the olives and the
lemon twist.

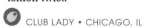 CLUB LADY • CHICAGO, IL

Club Macanudo

2 oz. Grey Goose vodka
½ oz. Lillet
Splash Grand Marnier
½ oz. champagne to top

Shake the first three ingredients with ice, strain
into a glass, and top with the champagne.

 FERNANDO ALUARDO • CLUB MACANUDO •
CHICAGO, IL

Cobalt Blue Martini

2 oz. gin
⅛ oz. blue curaçao
Lemon twist for garnish

Cocoa-Banana Martini

Cocoa powder to rim
1 oz. vodka
½ oz. banana liqueur
½ oz. dark crème de cacao

Rim a martini glass with cocoa powder. Shake
with ice, and strain into the glass.

Code Red Martini

2 oz. Skyy vodka
¼ oz. cranberry juice
¼ oz. Grand Marnier
Twist for garnish

Shake with ice, and strain into a chilled martini glass. Serve straight up or on the rocks. Garnish with the twist.

Coffee Martini

2 oz. Kahlúa
⅛ oz. Disaronno amaretto
⅛ oz. sweet vermouth

Shake with ice, and strain into a chilled martini glass. Serve on the rocks or straight up.

Cointini

2 oz. Stolichnaya Ohranj vodka
⅛ oz. Cointreau liqueur

Shake with ice, and strain into a chilled martini glass. Serve on the rocks or straight up.

 BRASSERIE JO • CHICAGO, IL

Cold Deck Martini

1 ½ oz. brandy
¾ oz. Martini & Rossi Rosso sweet vermouth
¼ oz. crème de menthe

Shake with ice, and strain into a chilled glass.

Comfortable Possession

½ oz. Absolut Citron vodka
½ oz. Southern Comfort
Lemon twist for garnish

Shake with ice, and strain into a glass. Garnish
with the lemon twist.

Contemporary Martini

2 oz. Absolut Citron vodka
4 drops Cointreau
Orange peel for garnish

Shake with ice until well chilled, and strain into a
martini glass. Garnish with the orange peel.

 TOP OF THE HUB • BOSTON, MA

Continental Martini

2 ½ oz. Stolichnaya vodka
⅛ oz. Martini & Rossi extra dry vermouth
Lemon-stuffed olive for garnish

 THE CONTINENTAL CAFÉ • PHILADELPHIA, PA

Cool Blueberry Mint Martini

4 oz. Stolichnaya Blueberi vodka
2 oz. blueberry puree
1 oz. limoncello
Juice of ½ lemon
Blueberries for garnish
Mint leaves for garnish

Shake with ice, and strain into martini glasses. Garnish with the blueberries and mint leaves. Serves 2.

 RYA KAIDING • SMOKEJACKS RESTAURANT
• BURLINGTON, VT

Cooperstown Martini

1 oz. dry gin
¼ oz. French vermouth
¼ oz. Italian vermouth
Dash Angostura
Dash orange bitters
Mint sprig for stirring
Lemon twist for garnish

Stir liquids with the mint sprig, and garnish with
the lemon twist.

Copenhagen Martini

1 oz. aquavit
1 oz. dry gin
½ oz. dry vermouth
Green olive for garnish

Copper Illusion Martini

¼ oz. Campari
¼ oz. Cointreau
Orange twist for garnish

Serve in a martini mixing glass filled with ice.
Garnish with the orange twist.

 MICHAEL VEZZONI • THE FOUR SEASONS OLYMPIC
HOTEL • SEATTLE, WA

Coral Martini

2 oz. Smirnoff citrus vodka
⅓ oz. freshly squeezed orange juice
Chilled champagne to top
Orange wheel for garnish

Shake the first two ingredients with ice, and strain into a martini glass. Top with chilled champagne. Garnish with the orange wheel.

Corkscrew Martini

1 ½ oz. light rum
½ oz. dry vermouth
½ oz. peach-flavored liqueur or brandy
Lime slice for garnish

Shake with ice, and strain into a chilled glass. Garnish with the lime slice.

Cornet Martini

1 ½ oz. Bombay Sapphire gin
Dash port wine
Lemon twist or olives for garnish

Stir with ice, and strain into a cocktail glass. Serve straight up or on the rocks. Garnish with the lemon twist or olives.

Cosmo Kazi

1 oz. cranberry juice
1 oz. Stolichnaya Citros vodka
½ oz. lime juice
½ oz. sweet and sour mix
½ oz. triple sec

Shake with ice, and strain into a glass.

 ALAN HARA • CLUB MIWA'S

Cosmo Limón Martini

2 oz. Bacardi Limón rum
¾ oz. cranberry juice
½ oz. Cointreau
¼ oz. Rose's Lime Juice
Lemon twist for garnish

Shake with ice, and strain into a chilled martini glass. Garnish with the lemon twist.

 SAFARI LOUNGE • FORT LEE, NJ

Cosmopolitan

2 oz. Bombay Sapphire gin or Stolichnaya
   Gold vodka
1 oz. cranberry juice
½ oz. orange liqueur
Splash fresh lime juice
Lemon twist for garnish

Cosmopolitan Martini

2 oz. vodka
1 oz. Cointreau
Juice from ½ lime
Splash cranberry juice
Twist for garnish

Shake with ice, and strain into a chilled martini
glass. Garnish with the twist.

Cosmopolitan Martini II

2 oz. vodka
¼ oz. blue curaçao
¼ oz. cranberry juice
Lemon twist for garnish

Shake with ice, and strain into a chilled martini glass. Serve straight up or on the rocks. Garnish with the lemon twist.

 SHERATON SEATTLE • SEATTLE, WA

Cosmopolitan Way Back When!

2 oz. vodka
¼ oz. Cointreau
¼ oz. cranberry juice
¼ oz. lime juice
Orange twist for garnish

Shake with ice, and strain into a chilled martini glass. Serve straight up or on the rocks. Garnish with the orange twist.

Cosmopolitini

2 oz. Absolut Citron vodka
½ oz. cranberry juice
¼ oz. Cointreau
⅛ oz. Rose's Lime Juice

Shake with ice, and strain into a chilled martini glass. Serve straight up or on the rocks.

 POLO LOUNGE • WINDSOR COURT HOTEL • NEW ORLEANS, LA

Cowboy Martini

2 ½ oz. Belvedere vodka
4 fresh mint leaves
Sugar to taste

Shake with ice and sugar, and strain into a chilled martini glass. Serve straight up or on the rocks.

Coyote Martini

1 liter tequila
3 serrano chiles

Add chiles to tequila in the bottle; let sit for 48 hours or more at room temperature. Put tequila in a freezer until thoroughly chilled. Serve straight from the freezer in chilled glasses.

 THE COYOTE CAFÉ • SANTA FE, NM

Cranberry Martini

1 oz. Absolut vodka
1 oz. cranberry juice
1 oz. Godiva original liqueur
Lime twist for garnish

Shake well with ice, and strain into a glass. Garnish with the lime twist.

Cranberry Sauce Martini

1 oz. Gordon's orange vodka
¼ oz. cranberry juice
Cranberries soaked in simple syrup for
    garnish

Crantini

2 ½ oz. Finlandia Arctic Cranberry vodka
¼ oz. Grand Marnier

Shake with ice, and strain into a chilled martini
glass. Serve straight up or on the rocks.

 PORTLAND'S BEST • PORTLAND, OR

Crantini II

2 oz. Bacardi Limón rum
Splash cranberry juice
Splash Martini & Rossi extra dry vermouth
Cranberries for garnish
Lemon twist for garnish

Shake, and serve straight up. Garnish with the
cranberries and lemon twist.

Crantini III

1 ½ oz. cranberry juice
1 ½ oz. Smirnoff vodka
Splash lime cordial
Lime wedge for garnish

Shake with ice, and strain into a glass. Garnish
with the lime wedge.

Crème Brûlée Martini

3 oz. half-and-half
1 oz. Kahlúa
1 oz. Stolichnaya Vanil vodka
Sweet powdered cocoa for garnish

Shake with ice, and strain into a chilled martini glass. Garnish with the sprinkle of sweet powdered cocoa.

Creole Martini

1 ½–2 oz. vodka
Dash dry vermouth, or to taste
1 small jalapeño pepper

Shake with ice, and strain into a chilled cocktail glass. Garnish with the jalapeño pepper.

Crown Jewels

2 ½ oz. Bombay Sapphire gin
½ oz. Chambord
Fresh red raspberry for garnish

Stir 50 times, and strain into a chilled martini glass. Garnish with the raspberry.

 CHARLIE RYDER, BEVERAGE DIRECTOR AND
SOMMELIER • LASALLE GRILL • SOUTH BEND, IN

Cruzan Flamingo

1 ½ oz. Cruzan Aged Light rum
1 ½ oz. pineapple juice
¼ oz. fresh lime juice
¼ oz. grenadine

Shake well with ice, and strain into a martini glass.

Csonka Martini

2 oz. Absolut vodka
½ oz. Chambord
Godiva raspberry chocolate for garnish

Shake with ice, and strain into a chilled martini glass. Serve straight up or on the rocks. Garnish with the chocolate.

 SHULA'S NO NAME LOUNGE • MULTIPLE
LOCATIONS IN FLORIDA

Cub Campari

1 oz. Absolut Kurant vodka
1 oz. Campari
½ oz. cranberry juice
½ oz. grapefruit juice

Shake with ice, and strain into a chilled martini glass. Serve straight up or on the rocks.

Cucumber Gimlet (Spatini)

½ oz. fresh lime juice
½ oz. simple syrup
2 ¼ thick slices of cucumber (seedless)
2 ½ oz. Hendrick's gin
Cucumber wheel for garnish

Muddle lime juice, simple syrup, and cucumber slices. Add gin. Shake vigorously, and strain into a martini glass. Garnish with the cucumber wheel.

 THE SEAGRAM BUILDING • NEW YORK, NY

Cucumber Martini

1 small sliced cucumber
2 ½ oz. Belvedere vodka
Lemon zest

Muddle the cucumber. Shake with vodka and lemon zest.

Curious George Martini

1 ½ oz. Smirnoff vodka
Splash banana liqueur
Shot cranberry juice
Banana wedge for garnish

Shake with ice, and strain into a glass. Garnish with the banana wedge.

Cyber Tron

2 ½ oz. Sobieski Cytron vodka
½ oz. cranberry juice
½ oz. Marie Brizard triple sec

Shake with ice, and strain into a chilled martini glass.

Czar

2 oz. Stolichnaya vodka
½ oz. Chambord
Lemon twist for garnish

Shake with ice, and strain into a chilled martini glass. Garnish with the lemon twist.

 ROBERT GAYLE • WHISPERS PUB • OVIEDO, FL

Czarina Martini

1 oz. Smirnoff black cherry vodka
Splash apricot brandy
Splash dry vermouth
Dash bitters

Shake with ice, and strain into a martini glass.

Czar's Strawberry Cup Martini

2 oz. Stolichnaya Razberi vodka
¼ oz. Godet Belgian white chocolate
   liqueur, chilled

Shake with ice, and strain into a chilled martini
glass. Serve straight up or on the rocks.

Damn the Weather Martini

1 ½ oz. gin
½ oz. fresh orange juice
½ oz. sweet vermouth
1 tsp. triple sec

Shake with ice, and strain into a chilled glass.

Damn the Weather Martini II

2 oz. Finlandia vodka
¼ oz. Chambord
⅓ oz. Veuve Clicquot champagne to top

Stir the first two ingredients with ice well,
and strain into a martini glass. Top with the
champagne.

 GEORGE DELGAO • WINDOWS ON THE WORLD
   • NEW YORK, NY

Dark Chocolate Martini

Mint leaves to rub and to garnish
2 oz. Smirnoff vodka
Splash dark crème de cacao

Rub a fresh mint leaf around the rim of a martini glass. Shake with ice, and strain into a glass. Garnish with the mint leaf.

Dark Crystal

2 ½ oz. Stolichnaya Cristall vodka
Splash Remy Martin VSOP
Lemon twist for garnish

Stir with ice, and strain into a glass. Garnish with the lemon twist.

 COMPASS ROSE • SAN FRANCISCO, CA

Dean Martini

2 oz. Ketel One vodka
Chilled olive for garnish
1 Lucky cigarette and a book of matches

Pour vodka into a cocktail glass, and garnish with the olive. Place the cigarette and matches on the side.

Dean's Martini

2 oz. Skyy vodka
¼ oz. Cointreau
¼ oz. cranberry juice
¼ oz. sweet and sour mix

Shake with ice, and strain into an oversized, chilled martini glass. Serve straight up.

Decadent Martini

1 ½ oz. Smirnoff vodka
Splash raspberry liqueur
Disaronno amaretto to float
Chocolate Kiss for garnish

Stir with ice, and strain into a glass. Float the amaretto, and garnish with the Chocolate Kiss.

Deep Sea Martini

1 ½ oz. gin
1 oz. Martini & Rossi extra dry vermouth
¼ oz. Pernod
Dash orange bitters
Lemon twist for garnish

Deitrich Martini

2 oz. Smirnoff vodka
Splash Campari
Splash dry vermouth
Orange peel for garnish

Shake with ice, and strain into a glass. Garnish
with the orange peel.

Delight of Dawn

1 ½ oz. Bombay Sapphire gin
½ oz. simple syrup
Dash cranberry juice
Dash rose water
Rose petal for garnish

Shake with ice, and strain into a martini glass.
Garnish with the rose petal.

 RYAN PECK • PRIME 108 RESTAURANT • UNION
STATION HOTEL • NASHVILLE, TN

Delmonico Martini

1 oz. dry gin
½ oz. cognac
½ oz. dry vermouth
½ oz. sweet vermouth
Dash Angostura bitters
Orange peel for garnish

Denise's Martini

1 oz. extra dry gin
⅙ oz. extra dry vermouth
Dash olive juice
1 small drop red food dye
Green olive for garnish

Shake with chipped ice, and strain into a martini glass. Add the extremely large green olive.

 DENISE NALYSNYK • CARPENTERSVILLE, IL

Depth Charge Martini

1 ¼ oz. gin
1 ¼ oz. Lillet
¼ oz. Pernod
Orange peel

Derby Martini

2 oz. Belvedere vodka
¼ oz. dry vermouth
Olive for garnish

Serve straight up or on the rocks. Garnish with
the olive.

 HOLLYWOOD BROWN DERBY • WALT DISNEY
WORLD, FL

Dernier Round Martini

1 ½ oz. dry gin
½ oz. vermouth
¼ oz. cognac
¼ oz. Cointreau
Dash Angostura bitters

Dew Barrymore

1 ¼ oz. Tulamore Dew Irish whiskey
1 oz. sour mix
¾ oz. Raspberry Pucker

Shake with ice, and strain into a martini glass.

 ALAN SIGNOR • NEW YORK, NY

Dewey Martini

1 ½ oz. Absolut vodka
Dash Martini & Rossi extra dry vermouth
Dash orange bitters

Shake with ice, and strain into a cocktail glass.
Serve straight up or on the rocks.

Diablo Martini

1 ½ oz. white port
1 oz. dry vermouth
¼ tsp. fresh lemon juice
Lemon twist for garnish

Shake with ice, and strain into a chilled glass.
Garnish with the lemon twist.

Diamond Head Martini

2 oz. pineapple juice
1 ½ oz. gin
½ oz. curaçao or triple sec
1 tsp. sweet vermouth
Pineapple wedge for garnish

Shake, and strain into a glass. Garnish with the
pineapple wedge.

Diamonds Are Forever

2 ½ oz. Bombay Sapphire gin
Splash scotch
Olives for garnish

Stir with ice, and strain into a well-chilled martini glass. Garnish with the olives.

 GERARD LOUNGE • THE SUTTON PLACE HOTEL • VANCOUVER, BC

Diana Martini

1 ½ oz. Tanqueray gin
¾ oz. Martini & Rossi extra dry vermouth
¼ oz. Martini & Rossi Rosso sweet vermouth
¼ oz. Pernod
Lemon twist for garnish

Dick St. Claire's

2 ½ oz. Ketel One vodka
¼ oz. cherry heering
¼ oz. freshly squeezed lime juice
¼ oz. freshly squeezed orange juice

Shake with ice, and strain into a chilled martini glass. Serve straight up or on the rocks.

Diego Martini

2 oz. Smirnoff vodka
Splash Jose Cuervo Gold tequila
Dash orange juice
Orange wheel for garnish

Chill with ice, and strain into a glass. Garnish with the orange wheel.

Dillatini Martini

1 ½ oz. Absolut vodka
Dash Martini & Rossi extra dry vermouth
Dilly bean (if you can find one) for garnish

Shake, and strain into a glass straight or on the rocks. Garnish with the dilly bean.

Diplomat Martini

1 ½ oz. Martini & Rossi extra dry vermouth
½ oz. Martini & Rossi Rosso sweet vermouth
½ tsp. maraschino cherry juice
2 dashes Angostura bitters
Lemon twist for garnish
Maraschino cherry for garnish

Shake with ice, and strain into a chilled glass. Garnish with the lemon twist and maraschino cherry.

Dirty Martini

Lemon twist to rim glass
1 ¾ oz. extra dry vermouth
1 ½ oz. Bombay Sapphire gin
1 tsp. olive brine
Stuffed green olive for garnish

Rim glass with the lemon twist before pouring.
Shake with ice, and strain into a glass. Garnish
with the olive.

Dirty Sicilian Martini

2 ½ oz. vodka
Olive brine, to taste
Colossal Sicilian olives marinated in
    vermouth

Shake with ice, and strain into a chilled martini
glass. Serve straight up or on the rocks. Garnish
with the olives.

Dixie Martini

2 oz. dry gin
¼ oz. dry vermouth
¼ oz. Pernod

Dog Bites Back

1 ½ oz. bloody mary mix
1 oz. Skyy vodka
Lemon twist for garnish
Olives for garnish

Stir with ice, and strain into a chilled martini glass. Garnish with the lemon twist and olives.

 THE MARTINI CLUB • ATLANTA, GA

Don Shula Martini

2 ½ oz. Belvedere vodka
Cocktail mushrooms for garnish

Serve straight up, and garnish with cocktail mushrooms.

 SHULA'S NO NAME LOUNGE • MULTIPLE LOCATIONS IN FLORIDA

Dove Special

1 oz. Alizé
1 oz. Stolichnaya vodka
Orange twist for garnish

 MATT HOY • SWEETWATERS RESTAURANT • EAU CLAIRE, WI

Doyle's Dublin Martini (Boston Style)

2 ½ oz. Jameson Irish whiskey
½ oz. dry vermouth
3 drops Irish Mist
Lime rind for garnish

Pour into pint glass with ice cubes. Stir. Strain into a chilled martini glass. Add 3 leprechaun-size drops of Irish Mist. Garnish with a slice from the rind of a lime as green as a field of shamrocks.

 EDDIE DOYLE • BULL & FINCH PUB •BOSTON, MA

Dragon's Breath

2 oz. Bombay Sapphire gin
¼ blood orange, squeezed
¼ oz. Cointreau, flamed and poured into a glass
Splash Martini & Rossi extra dry vermouth
Clementine wedge for garnish

 900 WEST IN THE HOTEL VANCOUVER
• VANCOUVER, BC

Drambuie Bonnie Prince

1 ½ parts Bombay Sapphire gin
¼ part Drambuie liqueur
¼ part white wine
Orange peel for garnish

Shake with ice, and strain into a chilled martini cocktail glass. Garnish with the orange peel.

Drambuie Screamin' Hudson

1 ½ parts Canadian whisky
½ part Drambuie liqueur
½ part lemon juice

Shake with ice, and strain into a martini cocktail glass.

Dressed To "K"ill

2 oz. Ketel One vodka
Splash blue curaçao
Splash Grand Marnier
Splash orange curaçao
Splash soda
Maraschino cherry for garnish
Orange twist for garnish

Shake the first four ingredients well with ice. Add splash of soda, and strain into a chilled martini glass. Garnish with the maraschino cherry and orange twist.

 RIC STOROZUK • NORTHFIELD CTR., OH

Drew's Special

½ oz. half-and-half
¼ oz. amaretto
¼ oz. Baileys Irish cream
¼ oz. Chambord
¼ oz. Godiva original liqueur
¼ oz. Godiva white chocolate liqueur
¼ oz. Kahlúa
Chocolate syrup to decorate glass

Shake with ice, and strain into a chilled martini glass. Serve straight up or on the rocks. Drizzle chocolate over the glass.

 DREW SCOTT • LOMBARDI'S • ISSAQUAH, WA

Driest Martini

1 oz. Absolut vodka
1 oz. Tanqueray gin
Dry ice chunk for garnish

Stir with ice, and strain into a chilled cocktail glass. Garnish with the dry ice.

 BRIAN REA • GRASS VALLEY, CA

Dry Gem

2 ½ oz. Bombay Sapphire gin
⅛ oz. dry vermouth
Black olive for garnish

Shake with ice, and strain into a chilled martini glass straight up or on the rocks.

 RENAISSANCE ATLANTA HOTEL • ATLANTA, GA

Dry Martini

2 oz. dry gin
Splash dry vermouth
Green olive or twist for garnish

Shake or stir with ice, and strain into a glass. Serve straight up. Garnish with the green olive or twist.

Dry Martini (5-1)

1 ⅔ oz. gin
⅓ oz. dry vermouth
Lemon twist or olive for garnish

Stir with ice, and strain into a cocktail glass.
Garnish with the lemon twist or olive.

Dry Victoria Martini

3 oz. Bombay Sapphire gin
1 oz. Martini & Rossi extra dry vermouth
1 or 2 dashes orange bitters (or orange
   peel)
Cocktail olive for garnish
Lemon twist for garnish

Shake or stir with ice, and strain into a classic
martini glass. Garnish with the cocktail olive and
lemon twist.

Du Barry Cocktail Martini

1 ½ oz. dry gin
¾ oz. Martini & Rossi extra dry vermouth
¼ oz. Pernod
Dash Angostura bitters
Orange slice for garnish

Dubonnet Cocktail Martini

1 oz. Dubonnet Rouge
¾ oz. gin
Dash orange bitters
Lemon twist for garnish

Stir with ice, and strain into a chilled glass.
Garnish with the lemon twist.

Dusty Martini

Splash J&B scotch
2 oz. Smirnoff vodka, chilled
Olive for garnish

Pour several drops of scotch into the bottom of
a martini glass, and stir to coat. Shake out extra
scotch from the glass. Strain vodka into the martini glass. Garnish with the olive.

Dutch Chocolate Martini

2 oz. Leyden gin
1 ½ oz. crème de cacao
½ oz. lemon juice
½ tsp. grenadine

Shake with ice, and strain into a cocktail glass.

 JOE NACCI, BEVERAGE MANAGER/BARTENDER
• GIBSON'S RESTAURANT • CHICAGO, IL

Easy Like Sunday Morning

Chambord to rim
1 ½ oz. Grey Goose vodka
1 oz. Cointreau
½ oz. passion fruit sorbet
Champagne to float

Rim a glass with Chambord. Shake with ice, and strain into the glass. Float champagne on top.

 ROBERT CRANE AND PAMELA FRIEDMAN
• MISTRAL • BOSTON, MA

Eden Martini

1 ½ oz. Smirnoff vodka
Splash apple liqueur
Apple wedge for garnish
Cinnamon stick for garnish

Shake with ice, and strain into a glass. Garnish with the apple wedge and a cinnamon stick.

Egyptian Club Chocolate Martini

1 oz. Absolut vodka
1 oz. Godiva original liqueur
½ oz. Baileys Irish cream
Chocolate-covered maraschino cherry for
  garnish

Shake with ice, and strain into a chilled martini
glass. Garnish with the maraschino cherry.

 KIMBERLY DAVIS • THE EGYPTIAN CLUB •
PORTLAND, OR

El Martini Patrón

2 ½ oz. Patrón Añejo
Hint lime juice
Hint triple sec

Shake with ice, and strain into a chilled martini
glass. Serve straight up or on the rocks.

 HURRICANE RESTAURANT • PASSAGRILLE, FL

El Presidente #1 Martini

1 ½ oz. tequila
¾ oz. Martini & Rossi extra dry vermouth
Dash Angostura bitters

Stir with ice, and strain into a chilled glass.

Electric Peach Martini

2 oz. Finlandia vodka, chilled
½ oz. cranberry juice cocktail
¼ oz. orange juice
¼ oz. peach schnapps

Shake with ice, and strain into a chilled martini glass.

Elegant Martini

1 ½ oz. Absolut vodka
¼ oz. Grand Marnier (plus dash to float)
Dash Martini & Rossi extra dry vermouth

Stir with ice, and strain into a glass. Serve on ice or straight up. Float Grand Marnier on top.

Emerald Martini

2 oz. Bacardi Limón rum
Splash Martini & Rossi extra dry vermouth
Splash Midori melon liqueur

Stir with ice, and strain into a glass. Serve straight up or on the rocks.

Enchanted Martini

1 oz. Encantado Mezcal
¼ oz. Martini & Rossi extra dry vermouth
1 jalapeño- or habanero-stuffed olive for
  garnish

Shake with ice, and strain into a martini glass.
Garnish with the olive skewered on a toothpick.

 MEZCAL IMPORTERS, INC. • NAPA, CA

Englewood Martini

1 oz. Stolichnaya Ohranj vodka
Splash Campari
Splash orange juice

Shake with ice, and strain into a chilled martini
glass.

 HEATHER PUSER • HILLSDALE, NJ

Environmintz

1 ½ oz. 360 vodka
½ oz. peppermint schnapps

Shake with ice, and strain into a chilled martini
glass. Serve on the rocks or straight up.

Escobar Martini

1 ¾ oz. tequila
¼ oz. dry vermouth
Green olive for garnish

Shake with ice, and strain into a chilled martini
glass. Serve straight up or on the rocks. Garnish
with the green olive.

Espionage Martini

1 ½ oz. Smirnoff citrus vodka
Splash white crème de menthe
Lemon twist for garnish

Shake with ice, and strain into a glass. Garnish
with the lemon twist.

Espresso Grande Martini

2 oz. Finlandia vodka, chilled
½ oz. Kahlúa
¼ oz. Grand Marnier

Shake with ice, and strain into a chilled martini
glass. Serve straight up or on the rocks.

Espresso Martini

2 oz. Stolichnaya Citros vodka
½ oz. Borghetti Caffe Sport espresso
    liqueur
Lemon twist for garnish

Espresso Martini II

2 ½ oz. Stolichnaya vodka
¼ oz. Kahlúa
¼ oz. Tia Maria
Coffee beans for garnish

Shake with ice, and strain into a chilled martini
glass. Serve straight up or on the rocks. Garnish
with the coffee beans.

 JOHN DOURNEY • IRONWOOD RESTAURANT •
BASKING RIDGE, NJ

Exterminator Martini

2 oz. Smirnoff vodka
½ oz. fino sherry

Chill, and strain into a martini glass.

Fabulous Martini

2 oz. Smirnoff vodka
Dash champagne
Purple grape for garnish

Shake with ice, and strain into a well-chilled martini glass. Top with a dash of champagne. Garnish with the grape.

Fantasio Martini

1 ½ oz. brandy
¾ oz. dry vermouth
1 tsp. maraschino cherry juice
1 tsp. white crème de menthe

Shake with ice, and strain into a chilled glass.

Fare-Thee-Well Martini

1 ½ oz. dry gin
½ oz. dry vermouth
¼ oz. orange curaçao
¼ oz. sweet vermouth

Farmer's Cocktail Martini

1 ½ oz. gin
¾ oz. dry vermouth
¾ oz. sweet vermouth
2 dashes Angostura bitters

Stir with ice, and strain into a chilled glass.

Fascinator Martini

1 ½ oz. Absolut vodka
Dash Martini & Rossi extra dry vermouth
Dash Pernod
Mint sprig for garnish

Stir, and serve straight up or over ice. Garnish with the mint sprig.

Faux Mint Julep

Small bag of fresh mint sprigs
2 ½ oz. Maker's Mark bourbon

Throw the fresh mint sprigs in the back of the fridge and forget them. Pour bourbon over ice.

Favorite Cocktail

¾ oz. apricot brandy
¾ oz. dry vermouth
¾ oz. gin
¼ tsp. fresh lemon juice

Shake with ice, and strain into a chilled glass on the rocks.

Feeney Martini

1 part crème de cacao (white or dark)
1 part Godiva liqueur (white chocolate or
    original)
1 part Stolichnaya Razberi vodka
Strawberry or Chocolate Kiss for garnish

Shake with ice, and strain into a chilled martini glass. Garnish with the strawberry or Chocolate Kiss.

 L'OPERA • LONG BEACH, CA

Fernet Branca Cocktail Martini

1 ½ oz. dry gin
½ oz. Fernet-Branca
¼ oz. sweet vermouth
Maraschino cherry for garnish

Ferrari Martini

2 oz. dry vermouth
1 oz. amaretto
Lemon twist for garnish

Stir with ice in a chilled glass. Garnish with the lemon twist.

Fibber McGee Martini

2 oz. dry gin
1 oz. fresh grapefruit juice
1 oz. Martini & Rossi Rosso sweet vermouth
3 dashes Angostura

Shake with ice, and strain into a glass.

Fifth Avenue Martini

1 ½ oz. dry gin
½ oz. dry vermouth
½ oz. Fernet-Branca

Fin de Siècle Cocktail Martini

1 ½ oz. dry gin
¾ oz. sweet vermouth
¼ oz. Amer Picon
Dash orange bitters

Final Approach

1 part Ron Rico rum
1 part vermouth
Lemon twist for garnish

 THE WINDSOCK BAR & GRILL • SAN DIEGO, CA

Fine and Dandy Martini

1 ½ oz. gin
½ oz. fresh lemon juice
½ oz. triple sec or Cointreau
Dash Angostura bitters
Maraschino cherry for garnish

Finlandia Blue Moon

3 oz. pineapple juice
2 oz. Finlandia vodka
¼ oz. blue curaçao
Orange zest for garnish

Finlandia Buff

2 oz. Finlandia vodka
½ oz. Baileys Irish cream
½ oz. Kahlúa

Shake with ice, and strain into a chilled martini glass on the rocks or straight up.

Finlandia Gold Digger Martini

2 oz. Finlandia vodka
2 oz. pineapple juice
¼ oz. Cointreau

Finlandia Lime Green Martini

2 oz. Finlandia vodka
1 oz. grapefruit juice
1 oz. Midori melon liqueur
Thinly sliced lemon twists for garnish
Thinly sliced lime twists for garnish

Finlandia Midnight Sun Martini

2 oz. Finlandia Arctic Cranberry vodka
1 oz. Kahlúa

Finlandia Naked Glacier

Superfine sugar to rim
2 oz. classic Finlandia vodka
¼ oz. peppermint schnapps

Rim a martini glass with superfine sugar. Shake
with ice, and strain into the glass.

Finlandia Topaz

2 oz. Finlandia vodka
½ oz. crème de caçao
½ oz. Frangelico

Shake with ice, and strain into a chilled martini
glass. Serve on the rocks or straight up.

Fino Martini

2 oz. dry gin
½ oz. fino sherry
Green olive or lemon twist for garnish

Shake with ice, and strain into a chilled martini
glass on the rocks or straight up. Garnish with
the green olive or twist of lemon.

Fire Alarm Martini

2 oz. Absolut Citron vodka
1 oz. tequila
Dash Tabasco sauce
1 small jalapeño pepper for garnish

Shake with ice, and strain into a chilled martini glass. Garnish with the jalapeño pepper.

 HEATHER PUSER • SMOKE • HILLSDALE, NJ

Fire and Ice Martini

2 oz. Smirnoff vodka, chilled
Chili pepper for garnish

Shake with ice, and strain into a martini glass. Garnish with the chili pepper.

Fire in the Hole

1 ½ oz. Bacardi rum
¾ oz. peppermint schnapps
2–3 dashes of Tabasco

Shake with ice, and strain into a chilled martini glass. Serve on the rocks or straight up.

Firecracker Martini

1 ½ oz. Captain Morgan Parrot Bay rum
⅔ oz. 7-Up
½ oz. grenadine
Orange juice to fill
Bacardi 151 to float

Shake the first three ingredients with ice, and strain into a glass. Fill with orange juice, and float Bacardi 151.

Firefly Martini

2 oz. Smirnoff vodka
¾ oz. grapefruit juice
Dash grenadine

Shake with ice. Serve on the rocks or straight up in a chilled martini glass.

Flamingo Martini

1 ½ oz. gin
½ oz. apricot brandy
½ oz. fresh lime juice
1 tsp. grenadine

Shake with ice, and strain into a chilled glass.

Flowers and Vines

1 ¼ oz. green Chartreuse
¾ oz. premium vodka
¾ oz. Chambord

Add the first two ingredients to a martini glass.
Dribble Chambord down the side of the glass to
settle at bottom.

 REBECCA GASS • BLUEBERRY HILL • ST. LOUIS, MO

Fluffy Duck Martini

1 ½ oz. advocaat liqueur
1 ½ oz. dry gin
1 oz. fresh orange juice
½ oz. Cointreau
Soda water to top

Mix the first four ingredients, and top with soda
water.

Flying Black Tie

3 oz. Grey Goose vodka
¼ oz. Campari
¼ oz. scotch
Pearl onion for garnish
2 black olives for garnish

Stir or shake with ice, and strain into a glass.
Garnish with the pearl onion on a toothpick in
the center of the two black olives.

 NELSON SOUZA • ASTOR HOTEL • MIAMI, FL

Flying Dutchman

1 ¾ oz. dry gin
¼ oz. Martini & Rossi vermouth
2 dashes orange curaçao

Shake with ice, and strain into a chilled martini
glass. Serve on the rocks or straight up.

Flying Dutchman II

2 oz. Beefeater gin
¼ oz. blue curaçao

Shake with ice, and strain into chilled glass.

Foggi Day Martini

2 ½ oz. Beefeater gin
¼ oz. dry vermouth
¼ oz. Pernod

Shake with ice, and strain into a chilled martini glass. Serve straight up or on the rocks.

 MAD 28 • NEW YORK, NY

Fore Play

1 oz. Captain Morgan's Parrot Bay Mango
1 oz. Captain Morgan's Parrot Bay Passion Fruit
½ oz. Captain Morgan's Parrot Bay Pineapple
½ oz. triple sec
Splash sour mix
Cranberry juice to fill
Splash Sprite
Pineapple slice for garnish

Shake the first six ingredients with ice, and strain into a chilled martini glass. Add splash of Sprite, and garnish with the pineapple slice.

 MELANIE LIEBERS • CAFÉ ONE 11 • JOHNSON CITY, TN

Fortunella Martini

¼ oz. Campari
1 oz. Ketel One vodka
¾ oz. Bombay Sapphire gin
¾ oz. Caravella
¼ oz. Cointreau
1 tsp. candied kumquat nectar for garnish
Lemon twist for garnish

Coat an ice-cold mixing glass with Campari, and
toss out excess. Add ingredients and shake with
ice. Strain into a chilled martini glass. Garnish
with the kumquat nectar and lemon twist.

 FOUR SEASONS OLYMPIC HOTEL • SEATTLE, WA

The Forty-Five

½ oz. bourbon
½ oz. Drambuie liqueur
½ oz. Martini & Rossi Rosso sweet vermouth
Dash vanilla extract
Dried cherry macerated in maraschino
    liqueur for garnish

Combine all ingredients in a cocktail shaker.
Add ice and stir quickly with a bar spoon for
10–15 seconds. Strain into a chilled martini glass,
and garnish with the dried cherry.

 C. HARDWICK • NEW YORK, NY

Four Alarm Martini

2 oz. Absolut Peppar vodka
1 oz. Patrón tequila
Dash Tabasco
1 small jalapeño pepper for garnish

Shake with ice, and strain into a chilled martini
glass. Garnish with the jalapeño pepper.

 HEATHER PUSER • HILLSDALE, NJ

Fourth Degree Martini

¾ oz. dry gin
¾ oz. dry vermouth
¾ oz. sweet vermouth
¼ oz. Pernod
Lemon peel twist for garnish

Stir with ice, and strain into a glass. Serve
straight up or on the rocks. Garnish with the
lemon peel twist.

Fragoli Martini

2 ½ oz. vodka
½ oz. Fragoli

Stir with ice, and strain into a chilled martini glass.

Framboise Martini

2 oz. Absolut vodka
¼ oz. Chambord
1 raspberry

 SAN YSIDRO RANCH • SANTA BARBARA, CA

Frangelico Martini

1 ¼ oz. Absolut vodka
½ oz. Tuaca liqueur
¼ oz. Frangelico

Stir with ice, and strain into a chilled martini glass.

 PRAVDA • NEW YORK, NY

Frank-A-Tini

2 ½ oz. Absolut Kurant vodka
Teeny-tiny touch of sweet vermouth and
    raspberries
Raspberries

Freeborn Floater

2 oz. Ketel One vodka
¼ oz. lime juice
Tomolives for garnish

Shake. Serve straight up or on the rocks in a chilled martini glass. Garnish with the Tomolives.

French Ginger Martini

2 oz. Domaine de Canton French Ginger
    liqueur
2 oz. vodka
½ oz. Cointreau

Serve in a chilled martini glass.

 JOHN COOPER • PHILADELPHIA, PA

French Horn

2 ½ oz. Absolut Kurant vodka
½ oz. Chambord
Twist for garnish

Shake with ice, and strain into a chilled martini glass. Serve on the rocks or straight up. Garnish with the twist.

French Kiss Martini

2 oz. Stolichnaya Ohranj vodka
¼ oz. Lillet

Stir gently with ice, and strain into a glass. Serve straight up or on the rocks.

French Martini

2 oz. Smirnoff vodka
Splash cognac

Shake well with ice, and strain into a martini glass.

French Martini II (aka Paisley Martini)

1 ½ oz. gin
¼ oz. scotch whiskey
Lemon twist for garnish

Shake with ice, and strain into a chilled martini glass. Serve on the rocks or straight up. Garnish with the lemon twist.

Fruit Burst Martini

½ oz. blue curaçao
½ oz. peach schnapps
½ oz. vermouth
½ oz. vodka
Pineapple juice to top

Place into shaker quarter filled with ice. Top with the pineapple juice. Shake, and strain into a shot glass.

 KEVIN HARE • BEDROCKS BAR & CASINO •
LOWER HUTT, NEW ZEALAND

Fruit of the Forest

2 oz. Wyborowa Swieza Lemon vodka
½ cup fresh summer berries

Shake with ice, and strain into a chilled martini glass. Serve on the rocks or straight up. Garnish with the berries.

Fruity Martini

1 ¼ oz. Gordon's grapefruit gin
1 ¼ oz. Stolichnaya Ohranj vodka
½ oz. Chambord

Shake with ice, and strain into a chilled martini glass.

Fudgesicle Martini

2 oz. Finlandia vodka, chilled
½ oz. crème de cacao
¼ oz. chocolate syrup

Shake with ice, and strain into a chilled martini glass. Serve on the rocks or straight up.

Fuzzy Fish Tini

1 oz. Black Haus schnapps
1 oz. peach schnapps
½ oz. cranberry juice
Splash sour mix

Shake with ice, and strain into a chilled martini glass.

 JIM DELFINO • MARTELL'S TIKI BAR • POINT PLEASANT BEACH, NJ

Fuzzy Gator

2 oz. Stolichnaya vodka
Splash Gatorade
Splash peach schnapps
Long lime twist for garnish

Fuzzy Martini

1 ½ oz. Smirnoff vodka
½ oz. peach schnapps

Chill, strain, and serve into a chilled martini glass.

Fuzzy Martini II

2 oz. Stolichnaya Vanil vodka
1 oz. Stolichnaya Peachik vodka
Splash peach schnapps
Thin peach slice for garnish

Shake with ice, and strain into a chilled martini glass. Serve on the rocks or straight up. Garnish with the peach slice.

Fuzzy Naval Martini

2 oz. Ketel One vodka
½ oz. freshly squeezed orange juice
½ oz. peach schnapps
Orange peel for garnish

Fuzzy Zinilla

3 oz. Stolichnaya Vanil vodka
1 oz. Stolichnaya Zinamon vodka
½ oz. peach schnapps
Orange twist for garnish

Shake with ice, and strain into a chilled martini glass. Serve on the rocks or straight up.

 GILBERT VALENTINE • LARKSPUR RESTAURANT & GRILL • WICHITA, KS

Galliano Moonbeam Martini

1 oz. Galliano
½ oz. Mezzaluna vodka
Lemon peel for garnish

Shake with ice, and strain into a martini glass. Garnish with the lemon peel twisted as a crescent moon.

 RYAN PECK • RAMADA PLAZA HOTEL • SHELTON, CT

Garden Martini

2 oz. Smirnoff vodka
3 drops dry vermouth
Cherry tomato for garnish
Pickled asparagus spear for garnish

Shake with ice, and strain into a glass. Garnish with
the cherry tomato and pickled asparagus spear.

Gazette Martini

1 ½ oz. brandy
¾ oz. sweet vermouth
1 tsp. lemon juice
½ tsp. sugar

Shake with ice, and strain into a chilled glass.

Gene Tunney Martini

1 ¾ oz. dry gin
¾ oz. Martini & Rossi extra dry vermouth
Dash lemon juice
Dash orange juice
Maraschino cherry for garnish

George's Way

2 ½ oz. Beefeater gin
¼ oz. dry vermouth
⅛ oz. Pernod

Shake with ice, and strain into a chilled martini glass. Serve straight up or on the rocks.

Georgetown Martini

2 ½ oz. Ketel One vodka
¼ oz. Grand Marnier
Orange slice for garnish

Shake with ice, and strain into a chilled martini glass. Serve straight up or on the rocks.

Georgia Peach

1 oz. Ketel One vodka
1 oz. orange juice
½ oz. peach schnapps
Peach slice for garnish

Stir with ice, and strain into a chilled martini glass. Garnish with the peach slice.

 THE MARTINI CLUB • ATLANTA, GA

Gibson Martini

2 ½ oz. Bombay Sapphire gin
Splash French vermouth
Pearl onion for garnish

Shake with ice, and strain into a chilled martini glass. Serve on the rocks or straight up. Garnish with the onion.

Gilroy Martini

1 oz. Beefeater gin
1 oz. cherry brandy
½ oz. dry vermouth
½ oz. freshly squeezed lemon juice
4 dashes orange bitters

Shake ingredients with ice, and strain into a chilled glass.

Gimlet Martini

1 ½ oz. Bombay Sapphire gin
Dash Rose's Lime Juice
Lime slice for garnish

Stir with ice, and strain into a cocktail glass straight up or on the rocks. Garnish with the lime.

Gin Aloha Martini

1 ½ oz. Bombay Sapphire gin
1 ½ oz. Cointreau
½ oz. unsweetened pineapple juice
2 dashes orange bitters

Shake with ice, and strain into a chilled glass.

Gin Cocktail

2 oz. Bombay Sapphire gin
2 dashes orange bitters
Lemon twist for garnish

Stir with ice, and strain into a chilled glass.
Garnish with the lemon twist.

Gin Crusta Martini

2 oz. dry gin
½ oz. Cointreau
½ oz. lemon juice
1 tsp. maraschino cherry juice
Dash Angostura bitters

Shake with ice, and strain into a chilled martini
glass. Serve on the rocks or straight up.

Gin N' It Martini

1 ½ oz. Beefeater gin
½ oz. Italian vermouth
Lemon twist for garnish

Shake with ice, and strain into a chilled martini glass. Serve on the rocks or straight up. Garnish with the lemon twist.

Gin Rush Martini

2 ½ oz. Leyden gin
½ oz. triple sec
3 dashes Angostura bitters
Lemon twist for garnish

Shake with ice, and strain into a chilled cocktail glass. Garnish with the lemon twist.

 JOE NACCI, BEVERAGE MANAGER/BARTENDER
• GIBSON'S RESTAURANT • CHICAGO, IL

Gin Sidecar Martini

2 oz. Beefeater gin
1 oz. Cointreau
1 oz. lemon juice

Shake with ice, and strain into a glass.

Gina's Chocolate Raspberry Martini

2 oz. Belvedere vodka
¼ oz. Chambord
¼ oz. dark chocolate liqueur
¼ oz. Martini & Rossi Rosso sweet vermouth
¼ oz. white chocolate liqueur
Fresh raspberry marinated in vodka

Shake with ice, and strain into a chilled martini glass. Serve on the rocks or straight up. Garnish with the raspberry.

 RHUMBA • CHICAGO, IL

Gin-Cassis Martini

2 oz. Beefeater gin
1 ½ oz. Hiram Walker crème de cassis
1 tsp. lemon juice

Shake with ice, and strain into a chilled martini glass. Serve on the rocks or straight up.

Ginger Martini

2 oz. Skyy vodka
⅛ oz. ginger
Dash sugar
Orange zest for garnish

Muddle ginger, and shake with vodka over ice.
Add a dash of sugar. Strain into a glass, and
garnish with the orange zest.

The Ginger Scot

1 ½ oz. Dewar's Blended scotch whiskey
¾ oz. Domaine de Canton French Ginger
    liqueur
Pinch freshly ground cinnamon

Stir ingredients with ice until nicely chilled, and
strain into a martini glass. Float a few sprinkles
of cinnamon on top.

Ginka Martini

1 ¼ oz. Bombay Sapphire gin
1 ¼ oz. Sobieski vodka
½ oz. Martini & Rossi extra dry vermouth
Lemon peel or green olive for garnish

Ginsational Martini

1 ½ oz. H. W. Schlichte Steinhäger dry gin
¼ oz. dry vermouth
Lemon twist for garnish
Olive for garnish

Ginseng Martini

1 American ginseng root
1 bottle vodka
Splash dry vermouth
Ginger slice for garnish

Add ginseng root to vodka and let stand for
two days. Once vodka is infused with ginseng,
add desired amount to a martini glass with
a splash of dry vermouth. Garnish with the
ginger slice.

 LE COLONIAL • WEST HOLLYWOOD, CA

Ginwin Martini

1 oz. Absolut Citron vodka
1 oz. Absolut Kurant vodka
¼ oz. Grand Marnier
Twist for garnish

Shake with ice, and strain into a chilled martini glass. Serve on the rocks or straight up. Garnish with the twist.

 JASON BOWERS • REGAS • KNOXVILLE, TN

Glacier Blue Martini

2 oz. Stolichnaya vodka
1 oz. Bombay Sapphire gin
¼ oz. blue curaçao

Shake with ice, and strain into a chilled martini glass. Serve straight up or on the rocks.

 OLIVER'S IN MAYFLOWER PARK HOTEL
• SEATTLE, WA

Glacier Mint Martini

2 oz. Smirnoff vodka
½ oz. peppermint schnapps

Strain into a chilled martini glass.

Glamorous Martini

2 oz. Smirnoff vodka
Dash grapefruit juice
Dash orange juice
Splash orange liqueur
Orange wheel for garnish

Shake with ice, and strain into a glass. Garnish
with the orange wheel.

Global Time

2 ½ oz. Tanqueray gin
¼ oz. Chambord
Lemon twist for garnish

Shake with ice, and strain into a chilled martini
glass. Serve straight up or on the rocks. Garnish
with the lemon twist.

 THE WINDSOCK BAR & GRILL • SAN DIEGO, CA

Gloom Chaser Martini

1 ½ oz. Bombay Sapphire gin
½ oz. Martini & Rossi vermouth
2 dashes grenadine
2 dashes Pernod

Shake with ice, and strain into a chilled martini
glass. Serve on the rocks or straight up.

The Godfather Martini

2 oz. Belvedere vodka
¼ oz. amaretto
¼ oz. Grand Marnier
¼ oz. Martini & Rossi extra dry vermouth
Maraschino cherry for garnish
Orange twist for garnish

Shake with ice, and strain into a chilled martini glass. Serve on the rocks or straight up. Garnish with the maraschino cherry and orange twist.

 HARRY'S VELVET ROOM • CHICAGO, IL

Godiva Apricot Martini

1 part Absolut vodka
1 part apricot brandy
1 part Godiva original liqueur
Maraschino cherry for garnish

Shake with ice, and strain into a chilled martini glass. Garnish with the maraschino cherry.

Godiva Black Currant Martini

1 oz. Godiva original liqueur
1 oz. Seagram's gin
¼ oz. crème de cassis
⅛ oz. lemon juice
⅛ oz. lime juice
Maraschino cherry for garnish

Shake with ice, and strain into a chilled glass.
Garnish with the maraschino cherry.

Godiva Cranberry Martini

1 oz. Absolut vodka
1 oz. cranberry juice
1 oz. Godiva original liqueur
Lime twist for garnish

Shake with ice, and strain into a chilled glass.
Garnish with the lime twist.

Godiva Mandarin Martini

1 oz. Absolut vodka
1 oz. Godiva original liqueur
Splash Cointreau
Orange slice for garnish

Shake with ice, and strain into a chilled glass.
Garnish with the orange slice.

Godiva Mint Martini

1 oz. Absolut vodka
1 oz. Godiva original liqueur
Splash white crème de menthe
Mint leaf for garnish

Shake with ice, and strain into a chilled glass.
Garnish with the mint leaf.

Godiva Naked Martini

1 oz. Absolut vodka
1 oz. Godiva original liqueur
Lemon peel or strawberry for garnish

Shake with ice, and strain into a chilled glass.
Garnish with the lemon peel or strawberry.

Godiva Nutty Martini

1 oz. Absolut vodka
1 oz. Godiva original liqueur
Splash Frangelico or amaretto liqueur
3 almonds for garnish

Shake with ice, and strain into a chilled glass.
Garnish with the almonds.

Godiva Raspberry Martini

Confectioner's sugar to rim
1 oz. Absolut vodka
1 oz. Godiva original liqueur
Splash Chambord or raspberry liqueur

Rim a martini glass with confectioner's sugar.
Shake with ice, and strain into the glass.

Godspeed Glenn Martini

3 oz. Bombay Sapphire gin
Splash Noilly Prat vermouth
Splash olive juice
Cocktail onion for garnish
Lemon twist for garnish
Olive for garnish

Shake well with ice, and strain into a glass.
Garnish with the onion, lemon twist, and olive
on a toothpick.

RENAISSANCE MAYFLOWER HOTEL •
WASHINGTON, DC

Gold Digger Martini

1 oz. Finlandia vodka
½ oz. Cointreau
½ oz. pineapple juice

Stir with ice, and strain into a glass. Serve straight up or on the rocks.

Gold Martini

2 oz. Stolichnaya vodka
¼ oz. Goldschläger
Lemon twist for garnish

Shake with ice, and strain into a chilled martini glass. Serve straight up or on the rocks. Garnish with the lemon twist.

Golden Girl Martini

1 ¾ oz. Beefeater gin
¾ oz. dry sherry
Dash Angostura bitters
Dash orange bitters

Shake with ice, and strain into a chilled martini glass. Serve on the rocks or straight up.

Golden Goose

1 ½ oz. Grey Goose vodka
½ oz. Grand Marnier
Splash orange juice
Orange zest for garnish

Shake with ice vigorously to make ice crystals
form. Strain, and pour into a frozen martini glass.
Garnish with the orange zest.

 JULIE GRANT • PUZZLES • ATLANTA, GA

Golden Martini

7 parts Gordon's Special Dry London gin
1 part French vermouth
Lemon twist for garnish

Shake with ice, and strain into a chilled martini
glass. Serve on the rocks or straight up. Garnish
with the lemon twist.

Golden Nugget Martini

2 oz. Smirnoff vodka
Dash hazelnut liqueur
Lightly roasted pine nuts for garnish

Shake with ice, and strain into a glass. Garnish
with the pine nuts.

Goldfinger

2 oz. Belvedere vodka
½ oz. Cointreau
⅛ tsp. edible gold dust
1 orange slice

Pour vodka and Cointreau over ice in a Boston shaker. Stir in gold dust and squeeze orange slice before adding to the shaker. Shake, and strain into a well-chilled martini glass. Garnish with the orange peel.

 GERARD LOUNGE • THE SUTTON PLACE HOTEL • VANCOUVER, BC

Golf Martini

1 ¾ oz. Bombay Sapphire gin
¾ oz. Martini & Rossi extra dry vermouth
2 dashes Angostura bitters

Shake with ice, and strain into a chilled martini glass. Serve on the rocks or straight up.

Goose Berry

1 ½ oz. Grey Goose vodka
1 oz. Godiva white chocolate liqueur
½ oz. Chambord
3 raspberries for garnish

Shake with ice, and strain into a chilled martini glass. Garnish with the raspberries.

 JASON SMITH • TAVERN ON RUSH • CHICAGO, IL

Goose Berry II

2 oz. Grey Goose vodka
1 oz. DeKuyper Peachtree schnapps
Squeeze of fresh lime
Rose petals for garnish

Shake with ice, and strain into a glass. Garnish with floating rose petals.

 BRENDAN CARD AND JOSÉ CARSON • THE
BUBBLE LOUNGE • SAN FRANCISCO, CA

Goose D'etat Martini

2 ½ oz. Grey Goose vodka
¾ oz. Lillet
Brie-stuffed black olive for garnish

Shake with ice, and strain into a chilled glass.
Garnish with the olive.

 JOSEPH E. MOORHEAD • BLACKHAWK LODGE •
CHICAGO, IL

Goose the Monk Martini

2 oz. Grey Goose vodka
Drop Chartreuse
Twist for garnish

Shake over ice, and strain into a glass. Set flame
to it, and garnish with the twist.

 ROBERT STURDEVANT • CAPITAL GRILLE •
BOSTON, MA

Gordon's Continental Martini

2 oz. Gordon's vodka
⅛ oz. Martini & Rossi extra dry vermouth
Lemon-stuffed olive for garnish

Shake with ice, and strain into a chilled martini
glass. Serve on the rocks or straight up. Garnish
with the lemon-stuffed olive.

Gordon's Cup Martini

2 oz. Gordon's Special Dry London gin
1 oz. port wine
7-Up or fizzy lemonade to top
Cucumber rounds for garnish
Lemon rounds for garnish
Mint sprig for garnish (in season)

Pour the first two ingredients on the rocks in
a tall glass. Top with 7-Up or fizzy lemonade.
Garnish with the cucumber and lemon or mint
sprig in season.

Gotham

2 oz. Smirnoff vodka
¼ oz. Campari
Olive trio for garnish

Shake with ice, and strain into a chilled martini
glass. Serve straight up or on the rocks. Garnish
with the olives.

Gran Martini

2 oz. vodka
½ oz. Grand Marnier
Lemon or orange twist for garnish

Stir with ice, and strain into a chilled martini
glass. Garnish with the lemon or orange twist.

 BOB PHILLIPS • MESSINA'S @ THE CROSSROADS

Gran Razgarita

2 oz. Gran Centenario Añejo tequila
¼ oz. Chambord
¼ oz. fresh lemon juice

Shake with ice, and strain into a chilled martini
glass.

 THE PEN-TOP BAR & TERRACE • THE PENINSULA
• NEW YORK, NY

Grand Crantini

2 oz. Finlandia Arctic Cranberry vodka

Serve chilled.

Grand Martini

1 ½ oz. Smirnoff vodka
¼ oz. Cointreau
¼ oz. orange juice
Orange peel for garnish

Stir with ice, and strain into a glass. Garnish with
the orange peel.

Grand Martini II

2 ½ oz. Stolichnaya vodka
¼ oz. Grand Marnier
Orange twist for garnish

Shake with ice, and strain into a chilled martini
glass. Serve straight up or on the rocks.

 RENAISSANCE ATLANTA HOTEL • ATLANTA, GA

Grand Obsession

2 oz. Absolut Kurant vodka
½ oz. cranberry juice
¼ oz. Grand Marnier

Shake with ice, and strain into a chilled martini glass. Serve straight up or on the rocks.

Grand Vodka Martini

2 ¼ oz. Ketel One vodka
¼ oz. Grand Marnier
Orange slice for garnish

Stir with ice, and strain into a chilled martini glass. Garnish with the orange slice.

 THE MARTINI CLUB • ATLANTA, GA

Granny Goose

2 oz. Grey Goose vodka
¼ oz. Grand Marnier
Orange twist for garnish

Shake with ice, and strain into a chilled martini glass. Serve straight up or on the rocks.

Grappa Martini

2 oz. Stolichnaya vodka
½ oz. grappa di moscato
Olives for garnish

Shake with ice, and strain into a chilled martini
glass. Serve straight up or on the rocks. Garnish
with the olives.

Great Secret Martini

1 ¾ oz. dry gin
¾ oz. Lillet
Dash Angostura bitters
Orange peel for garnish

Shake with ice, and strain into a chilled martini
glass. Serve on the rocks or straight up. Garnish
with the orange peel.

Green Dragon

3 oz. vodka
1 ½ oz. Grande Absente
1 ½ oz. Midori melon liqueur
Maraschino cherry for garnish

Shake until very cold, and strain into a chilled
martini glass. Garnish with the cherry.

Green Hornet Martini

2 oz. Finlandia vodka, chilled
½ oz. sweet and sour mix
¼ oz. Midori melon liqueur

Shake with ice, and strain into a chilled martini glass. Serve straight up or on the rocks.

Green Lantern Martini

1 ½ oz. vodka
¼ oz. lime juice
¼ oz. Midori melon liqueur
Lemon twist for garnish

Blend with ice, and stir. Garnish with the lemon twist.

Green Martini

1 ¼ oz. Stolichnaya Ohranj vodka
½ oz. Midori melon liqueur
3 splashes extra dry vermouth
Lemon twist for garnish

Shake well with ice, and strain into a martini glass. Garnish with the lemon twist.

 JANE LOMSHEK, BARTENDER • HOLIDOME • LAWRENCE, KS

Greenbrier Martini

1 oz. Bombay Sapphire gin
½ oz. Martini & Rossi vermouth
Lemon twist for garnish
Mint sprig for garnish

Greentini

2 oz. 360 vodka
½ oz. melon liqueur
Red Bull to top

Shake with ice, and strain into a chilled martini glass. Serve on the rocks or straight up. Top with Red Bull.

Grey Goose Passion

2 oz. Grey Goose vodka
½ oz. fresh passion fruit purée
Dash dry vermouth

Combine ingredients in a mixing glass. Stir gently. Strain into a chilled martini glass.

 ALBERT TRUMMER • DANUBE RESTAURANT & BAR • NEW YORK, NY

Grey Mare

2 ½ oz. Grey Goose vodka
Splash Gatorade Frost

Shake with ice, and strain into a chilled martini glass. Serve on the rocks or straight up.

 JAMES ZAZZALI • TARANTELLA'S • CLARK, NJ

The Griese Martini

2 oz. Skyy vodka
¼ oz. Godiva original liqueur
Hershey's Kiss for garnish

Shake with ice, and strain into a chilled martini glass. Serve on the rocks or straight up. Garnish with the Hershey's Kiss.

 SHULA'S NO NAME LOUNGE • MULTIPLE LOCATIONS IN FLORIDA

Grille Sunset Martini

2 ½ oz. orange juice
2 ½ oz. Skyy vodka
½ oz. Cointreau
Splash pomegranate juice
Maraschino cherry for garnish
Orange slice for garnish

Shake with ice, and strain into a chilled martini
glass. Serve on the rocks or straight up. Garnish
with the cherry and orange slice.

 SALT CREEK GRILLE • RUMSON, NJ

Guards Martini

1 ¾ oz. Beefeater gin
¾ oz. Martini & Rossi Rosso sweet vermouth
¼ oz. orange curaçao
Maraschino cherry or orange peel for
    garnish

Gumdrop Martini

Sugar to rim
2 oz. Bacardi Limón rum
1 oz. Belvedere vodka
½ oz. Southern Comfort
½ oz. sweet and sour mix
Mist of Martini & Rossi extra dry vermouth
3 tricolored gumdrops for garnish
Sugared lemon wheel for garnish

Rim a martini glass with sugar. Shake vigorously.
Garnish with your choice of three gumdrops and
a sugared lemon wheel.

 MAGNUM'S • CHICAGO, IL

Gunga Din Martini

2 oz. Bombay dry gin
¼ oz. Martini & Rossi extra dry vermouth
Juice of ¼ orange
Pineapple slice for garnish

Shake with ice, and strain into a glass. Garnish
with the pineapple slice.

Gypsy Martini

1 ½ oz. Bombay Sapphire gin
Dash Martini & Rossi extra dry vermouth
Maraschino cherry for garnish

Stir with ice, and strain into a glass. Serve straight
up or on the rocks. Garnish with the cherry.

H and H Martini

1 ¾ oz. Gordon's Special Dry London gin
¾ oz. Lillet
¼ oz. orange curaçao
Orange peel for garnish

Shake with ice, and strain into a chilled martini
glass. Serve on the rocks or straight up. Garnish
with the orange peel.

H.P.W. Martini

2 oz. Bombay Sapphire gin
¼ oz. French vermouth
¼ oz. Italian vermouth
Orange peel for garnish

Shake with ice, and strain into a chilled martini
glass. Serve on the rocks or straight up. Garnish
with the orange peel.

Hakam Martini

1 ¼ oz. dry gin
1 ¼ oz. Martini & Rossi Rosso sweet vermouth
¼ oz. Cointreau
Dash orange bitters
Maraschino cherry for garnish

Half & Half (French Kiss)

1 part Martini & Rossi extra dry vermouth
1 part Martini & Rossi Rosso sweet vermouth
Lemon or orange twist for garnish

Serve on the rocks, and stir well. Garnish with the
orange or lemon twist.

Half & Half Martini

2 oz. Bombay Sapphire gin
2 oz. Stolichnaya vodka
¼ oz. Martini & Rossi extra dry vermouth
Lemon twist for garnish

Shake with ice, and strain into a chilled martini
glass. Serve on the rocks or straight up. Garnish
with the lemon twist.

Hamlet's Martini

1 oz. Bombay Sapphire gin, iced
1 oz. Grey Goose vodka, iced
Splash Martini & Rossi extra dry vermouth
Cocktail onion for garnish

Shake with ice. Serve on the rocks or straight up
in a chilled martini glass. Garnish with the cocktail onion on a sword.

Hanalei Blue Martini

1 part blue curaçao
1 part Skyy Infusions Pineapple vodka

Shake and serve in an oversized martini glass.

Hanky Panky Martini

1 ¾ oz. Bombay Sapphire gin
¾ oz. Martini & Rossi Rosso sweet vermouth
¼ oz. Fernet-Branca
Orange peel for garnish

Harikiditini

1 ½ oz. shochu
Splash dry sake
Ume for garnish

Shake with ice, and strain in a glass. Garnish
with ume.

ALAN HARA • EMAILED TO OUR BLOG, WWW.
BARTENDERMAGAZINE.WORDPRESS.COM

Harold's Martini

3 oz. Gordon's Special Dry London gin
½ oz. Martini & Rossi vermouth
Dash orange bitters
Stuffed green olive for garnish

For those who never have more than one! Stir
and pour into a 6-oz. carafe. Bury the carafe in
shaved ice, and serve with a frosted cocktail
glass and a stuffed green olive.

JOHN F. BLUHG • EMAILED TO OUR BLOG, WWW.
BARTENDERMAGAZINE.WORDPRESS.COM

Harry's Martini

1 ¾ oz. dry gin
¾ oz. sweet vermouth
¼ oz. Pernod
Mint sprigs for garnish

Stir gently with ice, and strain into a glass.
Serve straight up or on the rocks. Garnish with
the mint sprigs.

Harry's Martini (San Francisco Style)

2 oz. Bombay Sapphire gin
¼ oz. green Chartreuse
Lemon twist for garnish

Shake with ice, and strain into a chilled martini
glass. Garnish with the lemon twist.

 HARRY DENTON'S STARLIGHT ROOM • SAN
FRANCISCO, CA

Hasty Cocktail

1 ¼ oz. Bombay Sapphire gin
¾ oz. Martini & Rossi extra dry vermouth
¼ oz. grenadine
Dash Pernod

Havana Club Martini

1 ½ oz. light rum
½ oz. Martini & Rossi extra dry vermouth

Shake ingredients with crushed ice, and strain into a chilled glass.

Hawaiian Cocktail Martini

2 oz. gin
½ oz. triple sec
½ oz. unsweetened pineapple juice

Shake with ice, and strain into a chilled glass.

Hawaiian Martini

1 ½ oz. gin
½ tsp. dry vermouth
½ tsp. pineapple juice
½ tsp. sweet vermouth

Mix all ingredients with cracked ice in blender. Strain into a chilled cocktail glass.

 VANIA THOMPSON • SPRINGFIELD, MO

Hazelnut Martini

2 oz. Gordon's vodka
½ oz. Frangelico
Orange slice for garnish

Shake with ice, and strain into a chilled martini glass. Serve straight up or on the rocks. Garnish with the orange slice.

Hennessy Martini

2 oz. Hennessy VSOP
½ oz. lemon juice
Lemon slice for garnish

Shake with ice, and strain into a glass. Garnish with the lemon.

Highland Fling Martini

2 oz. scotch
1 oz. Martini & Rossi Rosso sweet vermouth
2 to 4 dashes orange bitters
Green olive for garnish

Shake with ice, and strain into a chilled glass. Garnish with the olive.

Hi-Life Camomile Martini

1 ¼ oz. camomile tea–infused vodka
¼ oz. honey
Lemon peel for garnish

Infuse vodka with fresh camomile for 24 hours.
Take desired portion of vodka, shake, and strain
into a martini glass. Add the honey and garnish
with the lemon peel.

 MICHEL MOURACHIAN, MANAGER • KEVIN
CLAYBORN, MANAGER • BILL KENNY, GM • HI
LIFE • NEW YORK, NY

Hilliard Martini

1 ¼ oz. Bombay Sapphire gin
¾ oz. Martini & Rossi Rosso sweet vermouth
Dash Peychaud's bitters

Shake with ice, and strain into a chilled martini
glass. Serve on the rocks or straight up.

Hillsboro Martini

1 ¾ oz. dry gin
¾ oz. dry vermouth
Dash Angostura bitters
Dash orange bitters

Hoffman House Martini

¾ oz. dry gin
¾ oz. French vermouth
2 dashes orange bitters
Green olive for garnish

Hole-in-One Martini

2 oz. scotch
¾ oz. dry vermouth
¼ tsp. fresh lemon juice
Dash orange bitters

Shake ingredients with ice, and strain into a chilled glass.

The Holiday Martini

1 ½ oz. Absolut Kurant vodka
1 ½ oz. Finlandia Arctic Cranberry vodka
½ oz. Martini & Rossi Rosso sweet vermouth
Cherry for garnish

Shake with ice, and strain into a chilled martini glass. Serve on the rocks or straight up. Garnish with the cherry.

 HANDSHAKES BAR & GRILL • HOPEWELL JUNCTION, NY

194

Homestead Martini

1 ½ oz. Smirnoff Black vodka
Dash Martini & Rossi extra dry vermouth
Orange slice, muddled

Hong Kong Martini

2 parts dry gin
1 part French vermouth
1 tsp. lime juice
¼ tsp. sugar syrup
Dash Angostura bitters

Shake with ice, and strain into a chilled martini
glass. Serve on the rocks or straight up.

Honolulu Hurricane Martini

2 oz. dry gin
¼ oz. French vermouth
¼ oz. Italian vermouth
¼ oz. pineapple juice

Shake with ice, and strain into a chilled martini
glass. Serve on the rocks or straight up.

Hop Scotch

½ oz. Martini & Rossi extra dry vermouth
2 oz. Dewar's Blended scotch whiskey

Shake with ice, and strain into a chilled martini glass. Float scotch on top.

The Horton

2 ½ oz. Grey Goose vodka
⅛ oz. orange flower water

Shake with ice, and strain into a chilled martini glass. Serve on the rocks or straight up.

Hot Lips Martini

2 oz. Finlandia Arctic Cranberry vodka, chilled
¼ oz. Goldschläger

Shake with ice, and strain into a chilled martini glass. Serve straight up or on the rocks.

Hot 'N' Bothered Martini

2 oz. DeKuyper Peachtree schnapps
½ oz. vodka
¼ oz. DeKuyper Hot Damn! Burst

Shake with ice, and strain into a chilled martini
glass. Serve straight up or on the rocks.

Hot Potato

1 ½ oz. Glacier vodka
Dash Tabasco
Dash vermouth

Shake with ice, and strain into a chilled martini
glass. Serve on the rocks or straight up.

Hotzini

1 Charleston Hots pepper with pinholes
   (may substitute a serrano pepper)
2 oz. Ketel One vodka
1 fresh oyster on the half shell
¼ oz. caviar

Freeze a martini glass. Place 5 to 10 holes in the
pepper. Chill Ketel One vodka in a shaker glass
with the pepper. Pour into the frozen martini
glass. Remove the pepper from the shaker, and
put it in the martini glass. Present the glass on a
small plate, and garnish it with oyster and caviar.

 CHARLESTON PLACE • CHARLESTON, SC

Hula-Hoop Martini

2 oz. Finlandia vodka, chilled
1 oz. pineapple juice
½ oz. orange juice

Shake with ice, and strain into a chilled martini
glass. Serve straight up or on the rocks.

Iceberg Martini

2 oz. Beefeater gin
Splash white crème de menthe
Mint sprig or leaves for garnish

Stir with ice, and strain into a glass. Garnish
with the mint.

Ideal Martini

1 ½ oz. gin
1 oz. dry vermouth
1 tsp. unsweetened grapefruit juice
4 dashes maraschino cherry juice
Maraschino cherry for garnish

Shake with ice, and strain into a chilled glass.
Garnish with the cherry.

Idonis Martini

2 oz. Smirnoff vodka
1 oz. pineapple juice
½ oz. apricot brandy
Pineapple slice for garnish

Stir with ice, and strain into a glass. Garnish with
the pineapple slice.

Iguana

2 oz. Absolut Citron vodka
¼ oz. Midori melon liqueur
¼ oz. triple sec
Twist

Shake with ice, and strain into a chilled martini glass. Serve straight up or on the rocks.

Imperial Cocktail Martini

1 ½ oz. dry vermouth
1 ½ oz. gin
½ oz. maraschino cherry juice
2 dashes Angostura bitters
Maraschino cherry for garnish

Stir with ice, and strain into a chilled glass. Garnish with the cherry.

"In and Out" Martini

¼ oz. Martini & Rossi extra dry vermouth
2 oz. gin or vodka
Lemon twist or olive for garnish

Fill a shaker glass with ice, and add vermouth.
Swirl the ice around in the glass, and discard.
Add gin or vodka, and shake vigorously. Pour
into a cocktail glass. Garnish with the lemon
twist or olive.

 PATRICK FORD • SMITH & WOLLENSKY'S • NEW
YORK, NY

Inca Martini

1 oz. gin
½ oz. dry sherry
½ oz. dry vermouth
½ oz. sweet vermouth
Dash Angostura bitters
Dash orgeat syrup

Stir with ice, and strain into a chilled glass.

Indigo Blue Martini

2 oz. Skyy vodka
¼ oz. blue curaçao
Lemon twist for garnish

Shake with ice, and strain into a chilled martini
glass. Serve straight up or on the rocks. Garnish
with the lemon twist.

 BALLY'S • LAS VEGAS, NV

Indispensable Martini

1 ½ oz. dry gin
½ oz. French vermouth
½ oz. Italian vermouth
¼ oz. Pernod

Shake with ice, and strain into a chilled martini
glass. Serve on the rocks or straight up.

Inspiration

1 oz. Cork dry gin
¼ oz. Calvados
¼ oz. dry vermouth
¼ oz. Grand Marnier
Maraschino cherry for garnish

Mix, and garnish with the cherry.

International Martini

2 oz. Beefeater dry gin
¼ oz. Martini & Rossi extra dry vermouth
¼ oz. Martini & Rossi Rosso sweet vermouth
2 dashes crème de cassis

Irie Martini

2 oz. Bacardi rum
¼ oz. Grand Marnier
¼ oz. Tia Maria

Shake with ice, and strain into a chilled martini glass. Serve straight up or on the rocks.

Irish Martini

Cinnamon sugar to rim glass
2 oz. Tullamore Dew Irish whiskey
¼ oz. Baileys Irish cream

Rim a glass with cinnamon sugar. Shake with ice, and strain into the glass.

 CECILIA'S • BRECKENRIDGE, CO

An Irish Mexican in Russian Vanilla Fields

1 oz. Stolichnaya Vanil vodka
½ oz. Baileys Irish cream
½ oz. half-and-half
½ oz. Kahlúa
Scoop vanilla ice cream
Dash ground cinnamon

Mix all ingredients except cinnamon in blender.
Garnish with the cinnamon.

STEPHANIE MEAGHER-GARCIA • CHILLI'S BAR &
GRILL • MIAMI, FL

Iron Curtain Killer Kamikaze

2 oz. Stolichnaya vodka
1 oz. triple sec
2 lemon wedges
1 lime wedge
Double splash 7-Up
Splash tonic

ROB STYRON • SCARCELLA'S ITALIAN GRILLE •
TEMECULA, CA

Island Martini

2 oz. vodka (or gin)
¼ oz. blue curaçao
Orange slice for garnish

Shake with ice, and strain into a chilled martini glass. Serve on the rocks or straight up. Garnish with an orange slice speared with an umbrella.

 JILL STEVENS • TRABUCO CANYON, CA

It Ain't Easy Being Green

1 ¼ oz. 360 vodka
1 oz. half-and-half
¾ oz. chocolate liqueur
¾ oz. green crème de menthe

Shake with ice, and strain into a chilled martini glass.

Italian Ice Martini

2 oz. Smirnoff citrus vodka
Splash sweet and sour
Lemon twist for garnish

Pour into a glass with one ice cube, and garnish with the lemon twist.

Italian Martini

1 ½ oz. Frïs vodka
Dash of Hiram Walker amaretto

Shake with ice. Serve on the rocks or straight up in a chilled martini glass.

Italian Martini II

1 ½ oz. Bombay Sapphire gin
Dash Hiram Walker amaretto
Lemon twist or olive for garnish

Stir with ice, and strain into a glass. Serve straight up or on the rocks. Garnish with the lemon twist or olive.

Italian Martini III

2 oz. Belvedere vodka
½ oz. Frangelico

Shake with ice, and strain into a chilled martini glass. Serve straight up or on the rocks.

 MAD 28 • NEW YORK, NY

Italian Martini IV

2 oz. Artic (Italian) vodka
1 oz. Campari

Shake with ice, and strain into a chilled martini glass. Serve on the rocks or straight up.

Italia-Tini

2 oz. Stolichnaya vodka
¼ oz. amaretto

Shake. Serve straight up or on the rocks in a chilled martini glass.

Jack Frost Martini

2 oz. Smirnoff vodka
Peppermint schnapps to float
Peppermint candy stick for garnish

Chill and strain into a glass. Float peppermint schnapps, and garnish with the peppermint candy stick.

Jackie O Martini

1 ½ oz. Smirnoff vodka
Splash apricot brandy
Dash grenadine
Dash pineapple juice
Pineapple wedge for garnish

Chill, and strain into a glass. Garnish with the pineapple wedge.

Jackson Martini

1 ½ oz. Absolut vodka
Dash Angostura bitters
Dash Dubonnet

Stir with ice. Serve with ice or strain.

Jamaican Martini

2 oz. Absolut vodka
½ oz. Tia Maria

Shake with ice, and strain into a glass. Serve straight up or on the rocks.

James Bond Martini

3 parts Gordon's Special Dry London gin
1 part vodka
½ part Lillet
Lemon peel for garnish

Shake with ice until very cold, and strain into a chilled glass. Garnish with the large, thin slice of lemon peel.

Japanese Pear Martini

1 oz. fresh sliced pear
2 ½ oz. Belvedere vodka
Pear zest to top

Muddle the fresh pear, and shake it with vodka. Top with the pear zest.

Jazz Martini

2 oz. Bombay Sapphire gin
¼ oz. crème de cassis
¼ oz. lime juice

Shake with ice, and strain into a chilled martini glass. Serve on the rocks or straight up.

 MAD 28 • NEW YORK, NY

Jeremiah Tower's Startini

Splash Martini & Rossi extra dry vermouth
2 oz. Belvedere vodka
2 drops Edmond Briottet Mandarin liqueur
Orange zest for garnish

Rinse glass with Martini & Rossi extra dry vermouth. Stir with ice, and strain into a glass. Garnish with the orange zest.

 STARS • SAN FRANCISCO, CA

Jersey Lightning Martini

2 oz. Laird's Applejack brandy
1 oz. sweet vermouth
¾ oz. fresh lime juice

Shake with ice, and strain into a chilled glass.

Jet Lounge's Chocolate-Tini

1 ½ oz. Ketel One vodka
½ oz. Martini & Rossi extra dry vermouth
½ oz. white crème de cacao
Chocolate Kiss for garnish

 REEBOK SPORTS CLUB • NEW YORK, NY

Jewel Martini

1 oz. Bacardi Limón rum
⅛ oz. Midori melon liqueur (emerald)
⅛ oz. blue curaçao (sapphire)
⅛ oz. cranberry juice (ruby)

Layer in a martini glass.

 GATSBY • BOCA RATON, FL

Jockey Club Martini

1 ½ oz. Bombay Sapphire gin
⅓ oz. fresh lemon juice
¼ tsp. white crème de cacao
Dash Angostura bitters

Shake ingredients with ice. Strain into chilled glass.

Jose Cuervo Platino Margarita Martini

1 ½ oz. fresh lime juice
1 ½ oz. Jose Cuervo Platino
1 oz. simple syrup

Shake with ice, and strain into a chilled martini glass straight up.

Journalist Martini

1 ½ oz. Bombay Sapphire gin
¼ oz. Martini & Rossi extra dry vermouth
¼ oz. Martini & Rossi Rosso sweet vermouth
Dash Angostura bitters
Dash lemon juice
Dash orange curaçao

Shake with ice, and strain into a chilled martini glass. Serve on the rocks or straight up in a chilled martini glass.

Joy Jumper Martini

1 ½ oz. Smirnoff vodka
2 tsp. kummel
Splash lemon juice
Splash lime juice
Dash sugar
Lemon twist for garnish

Stir with ice, and strain into a glass. Garnish with the lemon twist.

Judgette Cocktail Martini

1 oz. Tanqueray gin
¾ oz. Martini & Rossi extra dry vermouth
¾ oz. peach brandy
1 tsp. fresh lime juice
Maraschino cherry for garnish

Shake with ice, and strain into a chilled glass.
Garnish with the maraschino cherry.

Jumpin' Jive Martini

1 ½ oz. Smirnoff citrus vodka
1 oz. pear liqueur
Dash peach schnapps
Splash cranberry juice
Splash lime juice
Pear slice for garnish

Shake with ice, and strain into a glass. Garnish
with the pear slice.

 BRENDAN LEE • RICHARD'S ON RICHARDS •
VANCOUVER, BC

Jungle Martini

1 oz. Beefeater gin
¾ oz. Martini & Rossi Rosso sweet vermouth
¾ oz. pineapple juice
¾ oz. sherry

Shake with ice, and strain into a chilled martini glass. Serve on the rocks or straight up.

Jupiter Cocktail Martini

1 ½ oz. Bombay Sapphire gin
¾ oz. Martini & Rossi extra dry vermouth
1 tsp. fresh orange juice
1 tsp. Parfait Amour or crème de violette

Shake with ice, and strain into a chilled glass.

Just Peachy

1 oz. Stolichnaya Peachik vodka
¼ oz. dry vermouth
Peach slice for garnish

Shake with ice, and strain into a martini glass. Garnish with the peach slice.

 PEGGY HOWELL • COTATI YACHT CLUB & SALOON • COTATI, CA

Kahlúa Dawn Martini

2 oz. dry gin
1 oz. Kahlúa
½ oz. lemon juice
Maraschino cherry for garnish

Shake with ice, and strain into a glass. Serve with the maraschino cherry.

Kangaroo Martini

1 ¾ oz. vodka
¾ oz. dry vermouth
Lemon twist for garnish

Kentucky Martini

2 oz. Orange Slice soda
1 ½ oz. Maker's Mark bourbon
½ oz. amaretto

Stir with ice, and strain into a glass.

Ketel One Cosmopolitan Martini

2 oz. Ketel One vodka, chilled
¼ oz. Cointreau
Hint cranberry juice

Shake with ice, and strain into a chilled martini
glass. Serve on the rocks or straight up.

 DIVISION SIXTEEN • BOSTON, MA

Key West Martini

2 oz. Malibu rum
½ oz. triple sec
3 splashes Rose's Lime Juice

Serve straight up in a martini glass.

The Keywester Martini

2 ½ oz. Bacardi rum
1 oz. cream of coconut
¾ oz. blue curaçao
Mist Martini & Rossi extra dry vermouth
Pineapple-stuffed cherry olive for garnish

Shake with ice, and strain into a chilled martini
glass. Garnish with the pineapple-stuffed cherry
olive, foil palm tree, sand, and blue water.

King Eider

2 oz. of your very best gin
1 oz. King Eider vermouth
Lemon twist for garnish

Mix, and garnish with the lemon twist.

 DUCKHORN VINEYARDS • ST. HELENA, CA

A Kiss from Mother Earth

2 oz. 360 Double Chocolate
3 oz. cream
1 oz. Agave Nectar
2 Pocky Sticks

Drizzle chocolate syrup in glass. Shake the cream and Agave with ice and strain into a martini glass. Garnish with two Japanese Pocky Sticks.

Kiss in the Dark

2 oz. Bacardi Limón rum
¼ oz. cherry brandy
¼ oz. Martini & Rossi extra dry vermouth

Shake with ice, and strain into a chilled martini glass. Serve straight up or on the rocks.

 STARS • SAN FRANCISCO, CA

Kiss Martini

Cinnamon sugar to rim
1 ½ oz. Smirnoff vodka
¼ oz. Baileys Irish cream

Rim martini glass with cinnamon-sugar mixture.
Shake with ice, and strain into a martini glass.

Kissin' in the Rain Martini

1 ½ oz. Rain vodka
½ oz. Marie Brizard Parfait Amour liqueur
Lemon twist for garnish

Chill, and strain into a martini glass. Garnish
with the lemon twist.

The Kiwi Martini

½ peeled and sliced kiwi
2 oz. Ketel One vodka
1 tsp. sugar

Muddle kiwi, and shake with Ketel One vodka
and sugar.

Knickerbocker Martini

1 ½ oz. dry gin
1 ½ oz. French dry vermouth
2 dashes orange bitters
Lemon peel for garnish

Stir with ice, and strain into a chilled martini glass. Garnish with the lemon peel.

 THE RAINBOW ROOM • NEW YORK, NY

Knickerbocker Martini II

1 ½ oz. Smirnoff vodka
Splash white crème de cacao
Dash Midori melon liqueur
Honeydew melon slice for garnish

Chill with ice, and strain into a glass. Garnish with the melon.

Kremlin Martini

2 oz. Smirnoff vodka
1 ½ oz. crème de cacao
1 ½ oz. half-and-half

Shake well with ice, and strain into a chilled martini glass.

K-Ting

2 oz. Ketel One vodka
¼ oz. Ting (a grapefruit soda imported
from Jamaica)

Shake with ice, and strain into a chilled martini
glass. Serve straight up or on the rocks.

 NICK AND EDDIE • NEW YORK, NY

Kurant Events Martini

1 oz. Absolut Kurant vodka
½ oz. Grand Marnier
Drop sweet vermouth
Splash cranberry juice
Raspberry for garnish

Shake with ice, and strain into a chilled martini
glass. Garnish with the raspberry.

 MICHAEL GOLONDRINA • MOROCCO SUPPER
CLUB • SAN FRANCISCO, CA

Kurant Martini

1 ¼ oz. Absolut Kurant vodka
Dash extra dry vermouth
Twist or olive for garnish

Shake or stir well with ice. Strain into a cocktail glass. Garnish with the twist or olive.

La Dolce Vita

2 ½ oz. Beefeater gin
½ oz. black sambuca

Shake with ice, and strain into a chilled martini glass. Serve on the rocks or straight up.

 BEAL HOUSE INN • LITTLETON, NH

Ladies' Choice Martini

1 ½ oz. Absolut vodka
¼ oz. kummel
Dash Martini & Rossi extra dry vermouth

Stir with ice, and strain into a glass.

Lady Godiva

2 oz. Smirnoff vodka
½ oz. Godiva original liqueur
¼ oz. white crème de cacao
⅛ oz. cocoa
Hershey's Kiss for garnish

Landing Martini

2 oz. Beefeater gin
¼ oz. Jose Cuervo Silver tequila
Twist for garnish

Shake with ice, and strain into a chilled martini glass. Serve straight up or on the rocks. Garnish with the twist.

 THE WINDSOCK BAR & GRILL • SAN DIEGO, CA

Last Round Martini

1 oz. Beefeater dry gin
1 oz. Martini & Rossi extra dry vermouth
¼ oz. brandy
¼ oz. Pernod

Shake with ice, and strain into a chilled martini glass. Serve on the rocks or straight up.

Last Tango Martini

1 ½ oz. Tanqueray dry gin
1 oz. orange juice
½ oz. Cointreau
½ oz. Martini & Rossi extra dry vermouth
½ oz. Martini & Rossi red vermouth

Shake with ice, and strain into a chilled martini glass. Serve straight up.

Lavender Citrus Cosmo

2 oz. Grey Goose L'Orange
1 oz. cranberry juice
¾ oz. Lavender Stirrings
½ oz. Cointreau
2 squeezes lime juice
Orange zest for garnish

Shake with ice, and strain into a chilled martini glass. Garnish with the flamed orange zest.

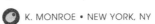 K. MONROE • NEW YORK, NY

Lawyer Liberation Martini

2 oz. Finlandia vodka
½ oz. grapefruit juice
¼ oz. Midori melon liqueur

Shake with ice. Serve on the rocks or straight up
in a chilled martini glass.

Le Ciel D'azur

2 oz. Skyy vodka
Splash blue curaçao

Shake with ice, and strain into a chilled martini
glass. Serve on the rocks or straight up.

 BRASSERIE JO • CHICAGO, IL

Leap Year Martini

1 ¼ oz. dry gin
½ oz. orange-flavored gin
½ oz. sweet vermouth
¼ oz. lemon juice
¼ oz. triple sec

Shake with ice, and strain into a chilled martini
glass. Serve on the rocks or straight up.

Lemon and Spice

1 oz. Absolut Citron vodka
1 oz. Absolut Peppar vodka
⅛ oz. dry vermouth
Lemon twist for garnish

Shake with ice, and strain into a chilled martini glass. Serve on the rocks or straight up. Garnish with the lemon twist.

 CECILIA'S • BRECKENRIDGE, CO

Lemon Chiffon Martini

2 oz. Finlandia vodka, chilled
1 oz. sweet and sour mix
¼ oz. triple sec
Lemon wedge

Shake with ice, and strain into a chilled martini glass. Squeeze and drop in the fresh lemon wedge.

Lemon Cosmopolitan Martini

2 oz. Absolut Citron vodka
½ oz. cranberry juice
Splash Sprite
Splash triple sec
Lemon twist for garnish

Stir with ice, and strain into a chilled martini glass. Garnish with the lemon twist.

 THE MARTINI CLUB • ATLANTA, GA

Lemon Drop Martini

Sugar to rim
2 oz. vodka
½ oz. fresh squeezed lemon juice
¼ oz. Cointreau

Rim a glass with sugar. Shake with ice, and strain into the glass.

Lemon Drop Martini II

Sugar to rim
Absolut Citron vodka
Splash lemonade
Twist for garnish

Rim a martini glass with sugar. Strain ingredients into the glass. Garnish with the twist.

 CECILIA'S • BRECKENRIDGE, CO

Lemon Drop Martini III

Sugar to rim
Stolichnaya Citros vodka
Squeeze fresh lemon

Rim a martini glass with sugar. Shake with ice, and strain into the glass.

Lemon Drop Martini IV

Sugar to rim
1 ½ oz. Absolut Citron vodka
¼ oz. sweet and sour mix
¼ oz. triple sec

Rim a martini glass with sugar. Stir vodka, sweet and sour mix, and triple sec with ice. Strain carefully into the martini glass.

 TONGUE & GROOVE • ATLANTA, GA

Lemon Grass Martini

½ oz. lemongrass
2 ½ oz. Belvedere vodka
Lemon zest

Muddle lemongrass, and shake with the vodka and lemon zest.

Lemon Meringue Skyy

1 ½ oz. Skyy Infusions Citrus vodka
½ oz. Carolans Irish Cream
Lemon to rim

Shake with ice. Serve in a lemon-rimmed, chilled martini glass.

Lemontini Martini

Splash Cointreau
2 oz. Stolichnaya Limonnaya vodka
½ oz. dry vermouth

Line a cocktail glass with Cointreau, and pour out excess. Stir with ice in a mixing glass, and strain into the cocktail glass.

Lenox Room Peachy Keen Martini

3 oz. peach nectar
2 oz. vodka
1 tsp. peach purée
Peach slice for garnish

Stir with ice, and strain into a chilled martini glass. Garnish with the peach slice.

 THE LENOX ROOM • NEW YORK, NY

Lew's Classic Martini

2 oz. Beefeater gin
⅛ oz. dry vermouth
Pimento-stuffed olive for garnish

Serve chilled and straight up. Garnish with the olive.

Liar's Martini

1 ½ oz. dry gin
½ oz. dry vermouth
¼ oz. orange curaçao
¼ oz. sweet vermouth

Stir gently with ice, and strain into a glass.

Licia Albanese Martini

1 ½ oz. dry gin
½ oz. Campari
Lemon twist for garnish

Shake with ice, and strain into a chilled martini glass. Serve on the rocks or straight up.

Lillet Cocktail Martini

1 ½ oz. Lillet
1 oz. dry gin
Lemon twist for garnish

Lime Drop

Sugar to rim
2 oz. Skyy vodka
⅛ oz. Cointreau
⅛ oz. lime juice

Rim a chilled martini glass with sugar. Shake with ice, and strain into the glass. Serve on the rocks or straight up.

Lime Light Martini

2 oz. Finlandia vodka
2 oz. grapefruit juice
½ oz. Midori melon liqueur
Lemon twists for garnish
Lime twists for garnish

Stir gently with ice, and strain into a chilled glass. Garnish with the thinly sliced lemon and lime twists.

Limón Crantini

2 oz. Bacardi Limón rum
½ oz. cranberry juice cocktail

Limón Martini

1 ½ oz. Bacardi Limón rum
½ oz. Martini & Rossi extra dry vermouth
Splash cranberry juice
Lemon twist for garnish

Shake with ice, and strain into a chilled martini glass. Garnish with the lemon twist.

Limón Twist

2 oz. Bacardi Limón rum
¼ oz. Cointreau
⅛ oz. Martini & Rossi extra dry vermouth
Lemon wedge for garnish

Limontini

2 oz. Stolichnaya Citros vodka
¼ oz. Cuantro
⅛ oz. dry vermouth

Shake with ice, and strain into a chilled martini glass.

Limontini II

1 ½ oz. Glacier vodka
½ oz. limoncello
Lemon wedge for garnish

Shake with ice, and strain into a chilled martini glass. Garnish with the lemon wedge.

Lindbergh Martini

1 oz. Absolut vodka
1 oz. peach schnapps
Splash orange juice
Orange peel for garnish

 THE WINDSOCK BAR & GRILL • SAN DIEGO, CA

Lobotomy Martini

1 oz. amaretto
½ oz. pineapple juice
¼ oz. Chambord

Shake with ice, and strain into a chilled martini glass. Serve on the rocks or straight up.

Locomoko

1 oz. cranberry juice
1 oz. orange juice
1 oz. Stolichnaya Ohranj vodka
½ oz. lime juice
½ oz. orange curacao
½ oz. triple sec

Shake with ice, and strain into a chilled martini glass. Serve on the rocks or straight up.

 ALAN HARA • CLUB MIWA'S

London Lemonade Martini

2 ½ oz. Bombay Sapphire gin
1 oz. fresh lemon juice
½ oz. Cointreau
½ oz. Rose's Lime Juice
Lemon twist for garnish

Shake with ice, and strain into a chilled martini glass. Serve on the rocks or straight up. Garnish with the lemon twist.

London Sun Martini

1 ½ oz. Beefeater dry gin
½ oz. dry sherry
Dash orange bitters
Twist

Shake with ice, and strain into a chilled martini glass. Serve on the rocks or straight up. Garnish with the twist.

L'orangerie Martini

2 oz. ice-cold Tanqueray Sterling vodka
¼ oz. Grand Marnier
Orange twist for garnish

Shake with ice, and strain into a chilled martini glass. Serve straight up or on the rocks. Garnish with the orange twist.

 OLIVER'S IN MAYFLOWER PARK HOTEL
• SEATTLE, WA

Lopez Martini

¾ oz. Absolut vodka
¼ oz. Disaronno amaretto
Lemon slice for garnish

Combine in a martini glass. Serve chilled or at
room temperature, straight up. Garnish with the
lemon slice.

 PIO LOPEX • MOM'S RISTORANTE • EDISON, NJ

Los Alto Martini

1 ½ oz. El Tesoro Silver tequila
1-2 dashes chardonnay
Lemon twist for garnish

Blend and stir. Garnish with the lemon twist.

Louis Martini

1 ½ oz. Bombay dry gin
½ oz. Martini & Rossi extra dry vermouth
¼ oz. Cointreau
¼ oz. Grand Marnier
Twist for garnish

Shake with ice, and strain into a chilled martini
glass. Serve on the rocks or straight up. Garnish
with the twist.

Louisiana Rain Martini

2 oz. Rain vodka
¼ oz. vermouth
Generous splash Louisiana Gold red
    pepper sauce
Red pepper for garnish (optional)

Shake with ice, and strain into a chilled martini
glass. Garnish with the red pepper (optional).

 RAIN VODKA • NEW ORLEANS, LA

The Love Martini

1 oz. Rain vodka, chilled
½ oz. white crème de cacao
¼ oz. Chambord

Serve in a chilled classic martini glass.

Loyal Martini

2 oz. Ketel One vodka
3 drops high-quality Balsamic vinegar

Stir gently with ice, and strain into a glass.

Lucien Gaudin Martini

1 oz. Bombay Sapphire gin
½ oz. Campari
½ oz. Cointreau
½ oz. dry vermouth

Lucky Mojo #99

2 oz. Stolichnaya Razberi vodka
½ oz. 99 Bananas liqueur

Chill over ice, and strain into a martini glass.

Lust for Life Cocktail

2 oz. Galliano
1 oz. fresh orange juice
½ oz. Marie Brizard Peach liqueur
Nutmeg for garnish

Shake with ice, and strain into a 5-oz. chilled martini glass. Serve on the rocks or straight up. Dust with nutmeg.

 JEFFREY BECKER • DELLA FEMINA RESTAURANT
• NEW YORK, NY

Luxury Martini

2 ½ oz. Belvedere vodka

Shake with ice, and strain into a chilled martini glass straight up.

Lychee Martini

5 lychee nuts
2 ½ oz. Belvedere vodka
Lime wedge, plus extra for garnish

Muddle lychees, and shake with Belvedere vodka and lime. Garnish with the lime wedge.

Maca Martini

1 oz. apple cider
1 oz. Sagatiba Pura Cachaça
1 oz. St. Germaine Elderflower liqueur
¼ oz. fresh lime juice

Shake with ice, and strain into a chilled martini glass.

 PRIVATE ROOF CLUB • GRAMERCY PARK HOTEL
• NEW YORK, NY

Mad 28 Martini

2 oz. Belvedere vodka
¼ oz. cranberry juice
¼ oz. Hine Vintage cognac
¼ oz. passion fruit juice

Shake with ice, and strain into a chilled martini glass. Serve on the rocks or straight up.

 MAD 28 • NEW YORK, NY

Madison Martini

2 ¼ oz. Bombay Sapphire gin
¼ oz. Dewar's Blended scotch whiskey

Add ice to a martini glass, and fill it with water. In an ice shaker, add scotch and gin, shake, and strain into a glass and drink.

 GREG HYDE • THE RIPPLE IN STILLWATER • EDNA, NM

Madras Martini

1 ½ oz. Finlandia Arctic Cranberry vodka
1 ½ oz. Stolichnaya Ohranj vodka
Orange twist for garnish

Put in a glass shaker filled half with ice. Stir with ice, and strain into a chilled martini glass. Serve on the rocks or straight up. Garnish with the orange twist.

 TOBY ELLIS • T.G.I. FRIDAY'S • CHEVY CHASE, MD

Mae West Martini

2 oz. Smirnoff vodka
Dash cranberry juice
Dash Disaronno amaretto
Dash Midori melon liqueur

Stir with ice, and strain into a chilled martini glass. Serve on the rocks or straight up.

Magic Martini

2 oz. milk
1 oz. Sobieski vodka
½ oz. Baileys Irish cream
½ oz. Kahlúa

Shake with ice, and strain into a chilled martini glass.

 FOGHORNS BAR N' GRILL • FAYETTEVILLE, AR

Magnificent Seven (with Lemon)

2 ¼ oz. Ketel One vodka
Splash cranberry juice
Splash Martini & Rossi extra dry vermouth
Splash sweet and sour
Splash triple sec
Sugar to rim glasses
Fresh lemons
Whole big dash of Love

 HI BALL LOUNGE • SAN FRANCISCO, CA

Maiden's Prayer

1 oz. Cork dry gin
½ oz. Cointreau
¼ oz. lemon juice
¼ oz. orange juice
Twist for garnish

Shake with ice, and strain into a chilled martini glass. Serve on the rocks or straight up. Garnish with the twist.

Maike's Papaya Sidecar

2 oz. Francet Cognac VS
1 oz. Grand Marnier
2 tbsp. fresh papaya puree
Squeeze fresh lemon
Lemon twist for garnish

Shake with ice, and strain into a martini glass. Garnish with the lemon twist.

Maker's Mark Martini

2 oz. Maker's Mark bourbon
Splash dry vermouth
Twist for garnish

Shake with ice, and strain into a chilled martini glass. Serve on the rocks or straight up. Garnish with the twist.

Malibu Martini

2 oz. Bombay Sapphire gin
½ oz. Malibu rum
⅛ oz. dry vermouth
Twist for garnish

Shake with ice, and strain into a chilled martini glass. Serve on the rocks or straight up. Garnish with the twist.

Malibu Rain Martini

2 oz. Finlandia vodka, chilled
1 ½ oz. pineapple juice
½ oz. Malibu rum
¼ oz. orange juice

Shake with ice, and strain into a chilled martini glass. Serve on the rocks or straight up.

Mandarin Martini

1 ½ oz. Stolichnaya vodka
1 oz. Bombay Sapphire gin
Dash Cointreau
Juice of ¼ mandarin orange
Mandarin orange section for garnish

Squeeze the juice of ¼ of a mandarin orange into the shaker with other ingredients (perfectionists should squeeze it through a tea strainer). Shake and strain into a martini glass. Garnish with mandarin orange.

Mandarin Pencil Sharpener Martini

2 oz. Bacardi Seven Tiki rum
¼ oz. Martini & Rossi Rosso sweet vermouth
¼ oz. sweet ginger syrup
Candied kumquat encased in pulled sugar
    for garnish
Gold flake and ginseng to fortify

Mandarin Sunset

1 ½ oz. Absolut Mandrin vodka
1 ½ oz. DeKuyper Watermelon Pucker
    schnapps
Splash orange juice
Orange slice for garnish

Mandarini

3 segments mandarin orange
1 ¾ oz. Absolut Mandrin vodka
Splash Cointreau
Splash sour mix

Muddle mandarin oranges in a shaker. Add ice
and other ingredients. Shake well, and strain into
a chilled martini glass.

 TONY M. KOZAR • RIVER CITY SALOON
• PORTLAND, OR

Mango 'Tini

¼ fresh peeled mango
2 oz. Belvedere vodka
⅛ oz. sugar

Muddle mango, and shake with the vodka and
sugar. Serve in a chilled martini glass.

Maple Leaf Martini

½ oz. amaretto
½ oz. banana liqueur
½ oz. cherry liqueur
½ oz. Midori melon liqueur
Splash cranberry juice
Splash grenadine

Shake with ice, and strain into a chilled martini glass. Serve on the rocks or straight up.

Maraschino Martini

2 ½ oz. Bombay Sapphire gin
¼ oz. cherry brandy
Maraschino cherry for garnish

Shake with ice, and strain into a chilled martini glass. Serve on the rocks or straight up. Garnish with the maraschino cherry.

Marcini

1 oz. Absolut vodka
1 oz. Jose Cuervo tequila
⅛ oz. extra dry vermouth
Lime wedge for garnish

Shake with ice, and strain into a chilled martini glass. Serve on the rocks or straight up. Garnish with the lime wedge.

 MARCIE JACKEL • WOODSIDE INN • TRENTON, NJ

Mardi Gras Skyy Martini

2 oz. Skyy vodka
½ oz. cranberry juice
⅛ oz. blue curaçao
⅛ oz. fresh lime juice
Twist for garnish

Shake with ice, and strain into a chilled martini glass. Serve on the rocks or straight up. Garnish with the twist.

Margit Martini

2 oz. Bombay Sapphire gin
½ oz. fresh lemon juice
Lemon twist for garnish

Serve chilled and straight up with a lemon twist.

Mariners Martini

¼ oz. Grand Marnier
2 oz. Ketel One vodka, chilled
Orange twist for garnish

Line a martini glass with Grand Marnier; swirl
and dump. Pour the vodka into the glass. Garnish
with the orange twist.

Marisa's "Outrageous Ohranj" Martini

1 ¾ oz. Stolichnaya Ohranj vodka
¼ oz. Cointreau
2 drops Martini & Rossi Rosso sweet
  vermouth
Orange peel for garnish

Shake with ice, and strain into a chilled martini
glass. Serve on the rocks or straight up. Garnish
with the orange peel.

MARISA SANTACROCE, BAR MANAGER
• SANTACROCES' ITALIAN RESTAURANT • HOOD
RIVER, OR

Maritime Martini

1 ½ oz. pineapple-infused vodka
½ oz. cherry-infused light rum
Maraschino cherry for garnish
Orange slice for garnish

Blend pineapple-infused vodka and cherry-infused light rum. Serve in a chilled martini glass, garnished with maraschino cherry and orange slice.

The Mark Hauser

2 oz. Ketel One vodka
¼ oz. Chambord

Shake with ice, and strain into a chilled martini glass. Serve on the rocks or straight up.

 THE DINER ON SYCAMORE • CINCINNATI, OH

Martian Gibson

2 oz. Grey Goose vodka
⅛ oz. scotch
Onion for garnish

Shake with ice, and strain into a chilled martini glass. Serve on the rocks or straight up. Garnish with the onion.

 JOHN CAINE • CAFÉ MARS • SAN FRANCISCO

Martinez Cocktail

Dash Boker's bitters
2 dashes maraschino
1 pony Old Tom gin
1 wine glass of vermouth
2 small lumps of ice

 JERRY THOMAS' BAR-TENDERS GUIDE 1887. THIS
COULD BE THE FIRST KNOWN MARTINI RECIPE.

Martini au Chocolate

2 oz. Stolichnaya Vanil vodka
¼ oz. Godiva original liqueur
Dusting cocoa for garnish

 BRASSERIE JO • CHICAGO, IL

Martini Avec Moi

1 shot Grande Absente
1 ½ oz. Remy Grand Cru VS
Splash crème de cassis
Splash Lillet Blonde
Lemon twist for garnish

Shake with ice until freezing cold. Strain into a
martini glass. Garnish with the lemon twist.

Martini Carib

1 ¼ oz. Cane Juice vodka
¾ oz. Key Largo schnapps
3 grapes for garnish

 STEPHEN DALE • BAHAMA BREEZE •
WINTER PARK, FL

Martini de Mure

2 ½ oz. Absolut Kurant vodka
¼ oz. crème de mure (blackberry liqueur)

Shake with ice, and strain into a chilled martini
glass. Serve on the rocks or straight up.

 BRASSERIE JO • CHICAGO, IL

Martini for Two—4.8 oz.

2 oz. Ketel One vodka or Beefeater gin
¼ oz. dry vermouth
Cocktail onions for garnish
Olives for garnish
Tomolives for garnish

Shake with ice, and strain into a chilled martini
glass. Serve with a plethora of cocktail onions,
olives, and Tomolives.

 SHULA'S NO NAME LOUNGE • MULTIPLE
LOCATIONS IN FLORIDA

Martini Jo

2 ½ oz. Stolichnaya vodka
¼ oz. Lillet Rouge
Orange twist for garnish

Shake with ice, and strain into a chilled martini
glass. Serve on the rocks or straight up. Garnish
with the orange twist.

 BRASSERIE JO • CHICAGO, IL

Martini "Manou"

2 oz. Stolichnaya Razberi vodka
¼ oz. Massenez Framboise Sauvage

Shake with ice, and strain into a chilled martini
glass. Serve on the rocks or straight up.

Martini Melon

2 oz. Finlandia vodka
½ oz. Midori melon liqueur
½ oz. orange juice

Martini Mint

2 oz. gin or vodka
1 oz. peppermint schnapps

Combine both ingredients in a mixing glass with ice cubes. Stir and strain into a chilled cocktail glass.

Martini Pernod

2 ½ oz. Beefeater gin
¼ oz. pastis—the cocktail of Provence

 BRASSERIE JO • CHICAGO, IL

Martini Picante

2 ½ oz. Absolut Peppar vodka
1 small jalapeño for garnish
Olive for garnish

Shake with ice, and strain into a chilled martini glass. Serve on the rocks or straight up. Garnish with the jalapeño and olive.

 SHERATON SEATTLE • SEATTLE, WA

Martini Refresher

1 ½ oz. gin
½ oz. dry vermouth
½ oz. sweet vermouth
1 drop peppermint extract
1-2 mint leaves for garnish

Combine over ice cubes in a mixing glass. Strain into a martini glass. Garnish with one or two mint leaves.

 JUDY BERNAS • TUCSON, AZ

Martini with a Kick

2 ½ oz. Absolut Peppar vodka
¼ oz. dry vermouth
Hot red chili pepper–stuffed olives for
   garnish

Maui Martini

2 oz. Smirnoff vodka
Splash blue curaçao
Splash Grand Marnier
Splash grapefruit juice
Lime twist for garnish

Maxim Martini

2 oz. dry gin
1 oz. Italian vermouth
2 dashes white crème de cacao

McKeegan's Dream

1 ½ oz. Bombay Sapphire gin (or Absolut)
¼ oz. Bushmills Irish whiskey

Shake with ice, and strain into a martini glass.

 NATIONAL BARTENDERS SCHOOL • LAKEWOOD, CA

Meat and Potato Martini

2 ½ oz. Teton Glacier Potato vodka
Splash dry vermouth
Sausage or pepperoni slice for garnish

Shake with ice, and strain into a martini glass.
Garnish with the slice of sausage or pepperoni.

 J & R'S STEAKHOUSE • CLAVERTON, NY

Mellow Yellow Martini

2 oz. Gilbey's gin
1 oz. Kina Lillet Blanc
1 drop Angostura bitters

Stir gently, and don't shake. Serve in a martini glass.

Melon Martini

2 ½ oz. Finlandia vodka
½ oz. Midori melon liqueur
Lemon twist for garnish

 BALLY'S • LAS VEGAS, NV

Melotini

1 oz. Martini & Rossi extra dry vermouth
½ oz. Midori melon liqueur
½ oz. pineapple juice
⅓ oz. lemon juice
Dash Angostura bitters
Lemon zest for garnish
Mint sprig for garnish

Mix in a stirring glass. Strain into an iced cocktail glass. Add a lemon zest and mint sprig.

 BOGDAN DADYNSKI • TRIER, GERMANY

Menthe

1 oz. Bombay Sapphire gin
1 oz. Martini & Rossi extra dry vermouth
¼ oz. white crème de menthe
Mint sprig for garnish

Shake with ice, and strain into a chilled martini glass. Serve straight up or on the rocks. Garnish with the mint sprig.

Meri Minti Martini

1 ½ oz. Baffert's mint gin
½ oz. Kahlúa
Mint sprig for garnish

Shake with ice, and strain into a martini glass. Garnish with the mint sprig.

 LORI JANEIRO WITH MARILYN CALLAHAN • LUCKY 7 CASINO • SMITH RIVER, CA

Mermaid

2 oz. pineapple juice
1 oz. Stolichnaya Ohranj vodka
¼ oz. blue curaçao
Pineapple chunk for garnish

Shake in a silver shaker, and strain into a glass.
Garnish with the pineapple chunk.

 MAUREEN & STEPHEN HORN • MERMAID MARTINI
BAR, SPIAGGIA, CAPE MAY, NJ

Mermaid Martini

2 oz. Absolut Citron vodka
½ oz. blue curaçao
½ oz. cranberry juice

Shake with ice, and strain into a chilled martini
glass. Serve on the rocks or straight up.

 FRED DEXHEIMER • BLT FISH • NEW YORK, NY

Mervyn-Tini

2 ½ oz. Stolichnaya Pertsovka vodka
¼ oz. dry vermouth
Caper berry

Shake with ice, and strain into a chilled martini
glass. Serve on the rocks or straight up.

Metropolis Martini

1 ½ oz. vodka
½ oz. strawberry liqueur
1 oz. champagne
Strawberry for garnish

Chill first two ingredients, strain, and top with champagne. Garnish with the strawberry.

Metropolis II

2 ½ oz Stolichnaya Razberi vodka
¼ oz. crème de framboise
¼ oz. raspberry eau de vie
Champagne to top

Metropolitan Martini

2 oz. Skyy vodka
½ oz. Fragoli Strawberry liqueur
Champagne to float

Serve straight up in an oversized, chilled stem. Shake, but do not stir. Float the champagne on top.

Mexican Cosmopolitan

2 oz. Ultimat vodka
1 oz. Patrón tequila
Splash cranberry juice
Splash lime juice

Shake with ice, and strain into a chilled martini glass. Serve on the rocks or straight up.

Mexican Ice Cube

2 scoops coffee ice cream
1 oz. Kahlúa
1 oz. orange juice
1 small can mandarin oranges (strained)
Orange slice for garnish

Mix ingredients in a blender until creamy. Pour into a shaker glass. Garnish with the orange slice.

 REID JUTRAS • OCTANE INTER LOUNGE • ROCKFORD, IL

Mexican Martini

2 oz. Smirnoff vodka
Dash Jose Cuervo Gold tequila
1 small jalapeño pepper for garnish

Layer in a chilled martini glass. Garnish with the jalapeño pepper.

Mexican Martini II

1 ½ oz. Gran Centenario Plata tequila
½ oz. extra dry vermouth
2-3 drops vanilla extract

Shake with ice, and strain into a chilled glass.

Miami Beach Martini

¾ oz. Dewar's Scotch Whiskey
¾ oz. Martini & Rossi extra dry vermouth
¾ oz. unsweetened grapefruit juice

Shake with ice, and strain into a chilled glass.

Miami Blue Moon

2 oz. Skyy vodka
¼ oz. blue curaçao
¼ oz. Grand Marnier

Shake with ice, and strain into a chilled martini
glass. Serve on the rocks or straight up.

Michael Collins Dublin Apple

2 oz. Michael Collins Irish whiskey
1 oz. DeKuyper's Sour Apple Pucker
  schnapps
Cranberry juice to top
Apple wedge for garnish

Shake over ice, and strain into a chilled martini glass. Top with cranberry juice, and garnish with the apple wedge.

 L. MOORE • SIDNEY FRANK CO. • NEW ROCHELLE, NY

Mickey Finn Martini

1 ½ oz. Absolut vodka
Dash Martini & Rossi extra dry vermouth
Splash Hiram Walker crème de menthe
  white
Mint sprig or leaves for garnish

Stir with ice, and strain into a glass. Garnish with the mint.

Midnight Martini

1 ½ oz. Echte Kroatzbeere Blackberry
   liqueur, chilled thoroughly
1 ½ oz. Teton Glacier Potato vodka

Shake with ice, and strain into a martini glass.

Midnight Martini II

1 ½ oz. Smirnoff vodka
Dash coffee liqueur
Splash orange liqueur
Orange wheel for garnish

Chill, strain, and garnish with the orange wheel.

Midnight Martini III

1 ½ oz. vodka
½ oz. Chambord
Lemon twist for garnish

Stir with ice, and strain into a glass. Garnish with
the lemon twist.

 GALLERY LOUNGE SHERATON • SEATTLE, WA

Midnight Sun Martini

2 oz. Finlandia Arctic Cranberry vodka
¼ oz. Finlandia Classic vodka
¼ oz. Kahlúa

Stir with ice, and strain into a glass.

Midori Spider's Kiss

Chocolate syrup
2 oz. Skyy vodka
1 oz. Midori melon liqueur
Juice from ½ lemon
Grenadine to drizzle

Draw a web on the side of a martini glass with the chocolate syrup. Chill glass. Shake with ice, and strain into the glass. Drizzle grenadine down the side for a blood effect.

Milano Martini

2 oz. gin
½ oz. Campari
¼ oz. dry Cinzano

Chill a glass of the gin, and pour in the Campari and Cinzano.

Mile High Martini

1 oz. Absolut vodka
1 oz. Skyy vodka
1 oz. Stolichnaya vodka
Olive for garnish

Shake and stir. Garnish with the olive.

 THE WINDSOCK BAR & GRILL • SAN DIEGO, CA

Milky Way Martini

2 oz. Ketel One vodka
¼ oz. Baileys Irish cream
¼ oz. Godiva original liqueur
Chocolate chips for garnish

 JOHN DOURNEY • EMAILED TO OUR BLOG, WWW.
BARTENDERMAGAZINE.WORDPRESS.COM

Minitini

2 oz. Bombay Sapphire gin
¼ oz. white crème de menthe

Shake with ice, and strain into a chilled martini
glass. Serve on the rocks or straight up.

 THE WINDSOCK BAR & GRILL • SAN DIEGO, CA

Mint Chocolate Kiss Martini

2 oz. Grey Goose vodka
1 oz. white crème de cacao
¼ oz. green crème de menthe
Chocolate stick for garnish

Shake over ice, and strain into a glass. Garnish
with the chocolate stick.

 PETE SAVOIE AND ADRYANN OMAR • TOP OF THE
HUB • BOSTON, MA

Mint Martini

½ oz. Absolut vodka
½ oz. Godiva original liqueur
Splash white crème de menthe
Mint leaf for garnish

Shake well with ice, and strain into a glass. Serve
straight up. Garnish with the mint leaf.

Mintini

1 ¾ oz. vodka
Splash Grand Marnier
Splash white crème de menthe
Maraschino cherry for garnish

Chill, and strain into a martini glass. Serve straight up. Garnish with the maraschino cherry.

 MIKE HENRY • PLANET HOLLYWOOD • ATLANTIC CITY, NJ

Mistico Martini

1 oz. Chambord
1 oz. Jose Cuervo Mistico
1 oz. sweet and sour mix

Stir with ice, and strain into a martini glass.

Mistletoe Martini

4 oz. Rain vodka
½ oz. Midori melon liqueur
Dash grenadine

Stir with ice, and strain into a glass. Add grenadine, which will descend to the bottom of glass.

 RAIN VODKA • FRANKFORT, KY

Mo Cocktail

2 ½ oz. Ketel One vodka
¼ oz. Chambord
5 squeezes lemon
Twist for garnish

Chill until very cold, and strain into a glass.
Serve straight up. Garnish with the twist.

Mobster

1 oz. Sobieski vodka
½ oz. Jägermeister
Herbs of choice for garnish

Shake with ice, and strain into a chilled martini
glass. Serve on the rocks or straight up. Garnish
with the herbs.

Mochatini

1 oz. Absolut Vanilla vodka
1 oz. dark crème de cacao
1 oz. Kahlúa Especial
Splash coffee

Chill, and strain into a frozen martini glass.

 BONNIE MCKESSON, BAR MANAGER • BOAR'S
HEAD SALOON • JULIAN, CA

Mochatini

1 ½ oz. Bacardi rum
1 ½ oz. Bacardi Seven Tiki rum
½ oz. Oblio Caffe sambuca
Dash Martini & Rossi extra dry vermouth

Shake with ice, and strain into a chilled martini
glass. Serve on the rocks or straight up.

 SHAW'S CRAB HOUSE • CHICAGO, IL

Modder Cocktail Martini

1 ½ oz. Gordon's Special Dry London gin
½ oz. dry vermouth
½ oz. Dubonnet
Lemon twist for garnish

Shake with ice, and strain into a chilled martini
glass. Serve on the rocks or straight up. Garnish
with the lemon twist.

Mojito Martini

Juice of ½ lime
1 tsp. sugar
Mint leaves
2 oz. white rum
Soda water to fill
Mint sprig for garnish

Place lime juice and sugar in a tall glass, and stir until sugar is dissolved. Rub mint leaves around the inside of the glass, and discard. Fill the glass with crushed ice, add rum, and stir. Top with soda water. Garnish with the mint sprig.

Monealize

1 oz. orange juice
1 oz. pineapple juice
½ oz. Alizé
½ oz. Southern Comfort
Maraschino cherry for garnish
Orange slice for garnish

Shake with ice, and strain into a highball glass. Garnish with the maraschino and orange slice.

Moneypenney

1 ¼ oz. Smirnoff vodka
Splash raspberry liqueur
Dash cranberry juice
Maraschino cherry for garnish

Chill, strain, and garnish with the maraschino cherry.

Monkey Bar's Banana Martini

2 ½ oz. Skyy vodka
½ oz. crème de bananes
½ oz. Martini & Rossi extra dry vermouth
Caramelized banana for garnish, sliced

Shake with ice, and strain into a chilled martini glass. Serve on the rocks or straight up. Garnish with the banana.

 REEBOK SPORTS CLUB • NEW YORK, NY

Monkey Business Martini

2 oz. Finlandia Arctic Cranberry vodka, chilled
1 oz. pineapple juice
¼ oz. Malibu rum

Shake with ice, and strain into a chilled martini glass on the rocks or straight up.

272

Monkey Shine Martini

2 oz. Finlandia Classic vodka
¼ oz. peppermint schnapps
Seltzer to top

Shake with ice, and strain into a chilled martini glass. Serve on the rocks or straight up. Top with the seltzer.

Montego Bay Martini

2 oz. Malibu rum
½ oz. Cointreau
⅛ oz. fresh lime juice

Shake with ice, and strain into a chilled martini glass. Serve on the rocks or straight up.

Montgomery Martini

3 oz. Gordon's Special Dry London gin
1 tsp. plus a few drops Noilly Prat vermouth
Olive for garnish

Montgomery Martini II

2 ½ oz. Tanqueray gin, chilled until ice-cold
⅛ oz. vermouth
Olive, twist, or onion for garnish

Montmartre Cocktail Martini

1 ½ oz. Bombay Sapphire gin
½ oz. Martini & Rossi Rosso sweet vermouth
½ oz. triple sec
Maraschino cherry for garnish

Shake with ice, and strain into a chilled glass.
Garnish with the maraschino cherry.

Moonshine Martini

1 ¾ oz. dry gin
½ oz. dry vermouth
¼ oz. maraschino cherry juice
2 dashes Pernod

Morgan's Martini

1 ½ oz. vodka
½ oz. Midori melon liqueur
Touch dry vermouth

 LARRY CLARK • MORGAN'S TAVERN •
MIDDLETOWN, VA

Morning Glory Martini

1 ½ oz. gin
1 oz. Stolichnaya Vanil vodka
½ oz. Calvados
Cinnamon stick for garnish

 CHRIS GOLZ • FORBIDDEN FRUIT • LONG BEACH, CA

Mosquito Martini

1 ½ oz. Sobieski vodka
⅛ oz. Cointreau
2 drops Tabasco sauce
Squeeze of lime wedge
Jalapeño for garnish

Stir with ice, and strain into a chilled martini glass. Garnish with the sliced jalapeño.

Mother's Day Martini

3 oz. Grey Goose vodka
Dash dry vermouth
Dash rose water
3 fresh rose petals for garnish

Stir gently, and strain into a chilled martini glass. Garnish with rose petals.

 ALBERT TRUMMER • DANUBE RESTAURANT & BAR • NEW YORK, NY

Moulin Rouge Martini

1 ½ oz. sloe gin
¾ oz. Martini & Rossi Rosso sweet vermouth
3 dashes Angostura bitters

Stir with ice, and strain into a chilled glass.

Moussellini Martini

2 oz. Bombay Sapphire gin
¼ oz. Tuaca
Lime twist for garnish

Serve chilled and straight up. Garnish with the
lime twist.

Mrs. Robinson Martini

1 ½ oz. Smirnoff vodka
Splash Galliano
Splash orange juice
Orange wedge for garnish

Stir with ice, and strain into a glass. Garnish with
the orange wedge.

Mud Puddle Martini

1 part Frangelico, chilled
1 part Rain vodka, chilled
Dash Kahlúa

Strain first two ingredients into a martini glass.
Add the dash of Kahlúa.

Muddy Waters

2 oz. Ketel One vodka
¼ oz. black sambuca

Shake with ice, and strain into a chilled martini
glass. Serve on the rocks or straight up.

Mumbo Martini

2 oz. Russian Roulette vodka
½ oz. olive juice
Splash dry vermouth
3 cocktail onions for garnish
3 small onions for garnish

 MUMBO JUMBO • ATLANTA, GA

Muscovy Neapolitan

1 part Stolichnaya Kafya vodka
1 part Stolichnaya Razberi vodka
1 part Stolichnaya Vanil vodka

My Personal Martini

2 oz. Frïs vodka
½ oz. Glen Deveron single malt scotch
    whiskey
15-year single malt scotch
Lemon twist for garnish

Serve straight up, very chilled, with the lemon twist.

 KASEN PRICE • EMAILED TO OUR BLOG,
WWW.BARTENDERMAGAZINE.WORDPRESS.COM

My Secret Goddess of Love

2 oz. Stolichnaya Razberi vodka
½ oz. Stolichnaya Peachik vodka
3 dashes grenadine
Splash cranberry juice
Splash pineapple juice
Dash orange juice

Shake with ice, and strain into a chilled martini glass. Serve on the rocks or straight up.

 IRIS VOURLATOS • EMAILED TO OUR BLOG,
WWW.BARTENDERMAGAZINE.WORDPRESS.COM

Myrna Loy Martini

2 oz. Smirnoff vodka
Splash Lillet
Orange peel for garnish

Shake with ice, and strain into a glass. Garnish with the orange peel.

Mysterious Jessy

1 oz. Stolichnaya vodka
½ oz. Baileys Irish cream
¼ oz. dark crème de cacao
¼ oz. Frangelico
Cherries for garnish

Shake with ice, and strain into a martini glass.
Serve straight up. Garnish with the cherries.

 ALEX REFOJO • CLUB MYSTIQUE • MIAMI, FL

Mystique Martini

2 oz. Smirnoff vodka
Dash Chartreuse
Lemon or lime twist for garnish

Chill, strain, and garnish with the lemon or
lime twist.

Napoleon Martini

1 ½ oz. gin
½ oz. Dubonnet Rouge
½ oz. Grand Marnier
Lemon twist for garnish

Blend and stir. Garnish with the lemon twist.

Naughty Martini

3 oz. cranberry juice
1 ¼ oz. Stolichnaya Razberi vodka
¾ oz. Midori melon liqueur
¼ oz. sour mix
Lemon wheel for garnish

Shake with ice, and strain into a chilled martini glass. Garnish with the lemon wheel.

Negroni Martini

2 parts gin or vodka
2 parts Martini & Rossi Rosso sweet
    vermouth
1 part Campari
Twist for garnish

Pour over ice, stir well, and strain into a glass. Garnish with the twist.

Nemo White Chocolate Martini

White chocolate to rim
2 oz. Grey Goose vodka
1 oz. Godiva white chocolate liqueur

Rim a glass with white chocolate. Pour with ice 3–4 times, and swirl. Strain into the glass.

 ADRIAN MISHEK • NEMO, MIAMI

Neon Martini

2 oz. Stolichnaya Ohranj vodka
½ oz. blue curaçao
½ oz. white crème de cacao
Orange twist for garnish

Shake with ice, and strain into a chilled martini glass. Serve on the rocks or straight up. Garnish with the orange twist.

Neve di Cervina

1 ½ oz. Disaronno amaretto
¼ tbs. honey
½ oz. whole milk
Dash ground cinnamon
Cinnamon stick for garnish

Stir amaretto and honey for 1 minute. Add ice and milk, and shake 30 times for the perfect froth. Strain into a chilled martini glass. Add a dash of ground cinnamon on the froth. Garnish with the cinnamon stick.

 NICK & STEF'S STEAKHOUSE • MADISON SQUARE GARDEN • NEW YORK, NY

New Yorker Martini

1 ½ oz. Martini & Rossi extra dry vermouth
½ oz. Beefeater dry gin
½ oz. dry sherry
Dash Cointreau

Shake with ice, and strain into a chilled martini glass. Serve on the rocks or straight up.

Newbury Martini

1 oz. Martini & Rossi Rosso sweet vermouth
1 oz. Tanqueray gin
¼ tsp. Cointreau
Orange slice for garnish

Shake with cracked ice, and strain into a chilled glass. Garnish with the orange slice.

Night Shift Martini

2 ½ oz. Bombay Sapphire gin
Splash Galliano
Olive for garnish

Stir with ice, and strain into a chilled martini glass. Garnish with the olive.

 CLUB 36 • SAN FRANCISCO, CA

Nightmare Martini

1 ½ oz. gin
½ oz. cherry brandy
½ oz. Madeira
2 tsp. fresh orange juice

Shake ingredients with ice, and strain into a chilled glass.

Nineteenth Hole Martini

1 ½ oz. Bombay Sapphire gin
½ oz. Martini & Rossi extra dry vermouth
½ oz. Martini & Rossi Rosso sweet vermouth
Dash Angostura
Black olive for garnish
Black flag

Stir with ice, and strain into a glass. Garnish with the black olive and flag.

Ninotchka Martini

1 ½ oz. Smirnoff vodka
½ oz. white crème de cacao
Splash lemon juice

Chill, and strain into a martini glass.

Nitelife Martini

1 ¼ oz. Absolut Mandrin vodka
1 oz. cranberry juice
¾ oz. Chambord
Splash 7-Up
Lime twist for garnish

Shake vigorously, and strain into a chilled martini glass. Garnish with the lime twist.

 R. OJA • NITE LIFE • BATON ROUGE, LA

No. 5

1 oz. Ketel One vodka
½ oz. amaretto
½ oz. Bacardi Limón rum
½ oz. Tuaca
2 drops Martini & Rossi extra dry vermouth
Rose petal for garnish

 RALPH VEGA III • THE PALACE NITE CLUB • EL PASO, TX

Nome Martini

7 parts dry gin
1 part dry sherry
Dash Chartreuse

Shake with ice, and strain into a chilled martini glass. Serve on the rocks or straight up.

Number 3 Martini

1 ¾ oz. Bombay dry gin
½ oz. Martini & Rossi extra dry vermouth
¼ oz. anisette
Dash Angostura bitters

Shake with ice, and strain into a chilled martini glass. Serve on the rocks or straight up.

Number 6 Martini

1 ¾ oz. dry gin
½ oz. Martini & Rossi Rosso sweet vermouth
¼ oz. orange curaçao
Lemon twist for garnish
Maraschino cherry for garnish
Orange peel for garnish

Shake with ice, and strain into a chilled martini glass. Serve on the rocks or straight up. Garnish with the lemon twist, maraschino cherry, and orange peel.

Nuptial Bliss Martini

1 ½ oz. Martini & Rossi extra dry vermouth
1 oz. Cointreau
1 oz. lemon juice
1 oz. orange juice
½ oz. kirsch

Shake with ice, and strain into a chilled martini glass. Serve on the rocks or straight up.

Nut House Martini

2 oz. Finlandia Arctic Cranberry vodka, chilled
¼ oz. amaretto

Shake with ice, and strain into a chilled martini glass. Serve on the rocks or straight up.

Nuttini Martini

2 oz. Smirnoff vodka
¼ oz. Disaronno amaretto
Orange wedge for garnish

Shake with ice, and strain into a chilled martini glass. Serve on the rocks or straight up. Garnish with the orange wedge.

Nuttini Martini II

2 ½ oz. Stolichnaya vodka
⅛ oz. Frangelico hazelnut liqueur
Orange twist for garnish

Shake with ice, and strain into a chilled martini glass. Serve on the rocks or straight up. Garnish with the orange twist.

Nutty Bacardi Spice Martini

2 ½ oz. Bacardi Seven Tiki rum
½ oz. hazelnut liqueur

Shake, and strain over ice. Serve straight up.

Nutty Martini

1 oz. Absolut vodka
1 oz. Godiva original liqueur
Splash Frangelico or amaretto liqueur
3 almonds for garnish

Shake with ice. Serve chilled. Garnish with the almonds.

Ohranj Martini

1 ½ oz. Stolichnaya Ohranj vodka
Dash Martini & Rossi extra dry vermouth
Splash triple sec
Orange peel for garnish

Shake with ice, and strain into a chilled martini glass. Serve on the rocks or straight up. Garnish with the orange peel.

Ohranj You Special

1 oz. Stolichnaya Ohranj vodka
Splash Grand Marnier
Shaved orange peel for garnish

 PEGGY HOWELL • COTATI YACHT CLUB & SALOON • COTATI, CA

Old Estonian Martini

1 ¼ oz. dry gin
1 ¼ oz. Lillet
2 dashes crème de noyeaux
2 dashes orange bitters
Orange peel for garnish

Old-Fashioned Martini

2 oz. Smirnoff vodka
Splash Martini & Rossi extra dry vermouth
Splash Martini & Rossi Rosso sweet vermouth
Lemon twist for garnish

Shake with ice, and strain into a chilled martini
glass. Serve on the rocks or straight up. Garnish
with the lemon twist.

Oliver Twist Martini

⅛ oz. dry vermouth
2 ½ oz. Beefeater gin to top

Dribble dry vermouth over ice in a rocks glass.
Strain. Add Beefeater gin to top.

 MR. G'S LOUNGE • DELTONA, FL

Oliver's Classic Martini

¼ oz. Cinzano dry vermouth
2 ½ oz. Bombay Sapphire gin or
  Stolichnaya vodka
2 large vermouth-marinated Italian olives
  for garnish

Pour vermouth into an empty martini mixing glass. Swirl to coat inside of glass, and dispose of excess. Fill coated glass with ice. Pour gin or vodka over ice, shake vigorously, and let stand 20 seconds. Strain mixture into the glass. Garnish with the olives.

 OLIVER'S IN MAYFLOWER PARK HOTEL
    • SEATTLE, WA

Oliver's Twist

2 ½ oz. Absolut Citron vodka
Lemon twist for garnish

 OLIVER'S IN MAYFLOWER PARK HOTEL
    • SEATTLE, WA

Olympic Gold

1 ½ oz. Absolut Citron vodka
1 oz. Bombay Sapphire gin
⅓ oz. Domaine de Canton French Ginger
   liqueur
⅙ oz. Martell Cordon Bleu cognac
Lemon twist for garnish

Shake with ice, and strain into a chilled martini
glass. Serve on the rocks or straight up. Garnish
with the lemon twist.

 MICHAEL VEZZONI • THE FOUR SEASONS OLYMPIC
HOTEL • SEATTLE, WA

Olympic Martini

1 ¾ oz. dry gin
½ oz. sweet vermouth
¼ oz. Pernod

Shake with ice, and strain into a chilled martini
glass. Serve on the rocks or straight up.

On the Runway

2 ½ oz. Stolichnaya Ohranj vodka
½ oz. orange juice
¼ oz. Campari
Orange twist for garnish

Shake with ice, and strain into a chilled martini glass. Serve on the rocks or straight up. Garnish with the orange twist.

On Time Martini

2 ½ oz. Bombay Sapphire gin
⅛ oz. vermouth
Olive for garnish

 THE WINDSOCK BAR & GRILL • SAN DIEGO, CA

One Exciting Night Martini

Sugar to rim
¾ oz. dry gin
¾ oz. Martini & Rossi extra dry vermouth
¾ oz. Martini & Rossi Rosso sweet vermouth
¼ oz. Sunkist orange juice
Lemon twist for garnish

Rim a glass with sugar. Mix, and serve in the glass. Garnish with the lemon twist.

Opera Martini

1 ½ oz. gin
½ oz. Dubonnet Rouge
1 tsp. maraschino cherry juice

Stir or shake with ice, and strain into a chilled glass.

Orange Delight

2 ½ oz. Stolichnaya Ohranj vodka
¼ oz. dark crème de cacao
Orange wedge for garnish

Orange Delite

2 oz. orange juice
1 oz. Stolichnaya Ohranj vodka
¾ oz. triple sec
½ oz. amaretto
Splash soda water

Combine first four ingredients over ice. Top with
a splash of soda water.

 LEE TEPFER • EMAILED TO OUR BLOG, WWW.
BARTENDERMAGAZINE.WORDPRESS.COM

Orange Martini

Orange peel to rub
2 oz. vodka
1 tsp. Grand Marnier
3 dried cherries for garnish

Rub the inside of a chilled martini glass with the orange peel. Shake vigorously with ice. Strain into the martini glass. Garnish with the dried cherries.

 TODD GREENO • NEW YORK, NY

Orange Martini Kick

2 oz. Stolichnaya Ohranj vodka
½ oz. sambuca
Orange rind to rim

Shake with ice, and strain into a chilled martini glass. Rub the rind of the orange on the rim of the glass.

 MIKE POLHAMUS • BENNIGAN'S • FAIRFIELD, NJ

Orange Mochatini

2 oz. Kahlúa
1 oz. Stolichnaya Vanil vodka
Splash chocolate liqueur
Splash orange liqueur
3 coffee beans or orange twist for garnish

Shake with ice, and strain into a chilled martini glass. Serve on the rocks or straight up. Garnish with the coffee beans or orange twist.

Orange Stinger

Sugar to rim
2 oz. 4 Orange vodka
¼ oz. white crème de menthe

Rim a chilled martini glass with sugar. Shake with ice, and strain into the glass.

Orange Truffle

2 oz. orange-flavored vodka
¼ oz. white chocolate liqueur

Shake with ice, and strain into a chilled martini glass. Serve on the rocks or straight up.

 THE VELVET LOUNGE • DETROIT, MI

Orangeberry 'Tini

2 ½ oz. Belvedere vodka
½ oz. orange juice
3 sliced strawberries
Orange slice or sliced strawberry for
    garnish

Shake fresh strawberries and orange juice with
Belvedere vodka. Pour into a chilled martini
glass. Garnish with the orange slice or a sliced
strawberry.

Orangesicle

2 ½ oz. 4 Orange vodka
½ oz. cream
Splash of orange juice

Shake. Serve in a chilled martini glass.

Orange-Tini

Orange peel to rim
2 oz. 4 Orange vodka
Splash Sunkist orange juice

Rim the glass with the orange peel. Shake with
ice, and strain into a chilled martini glass. No
fruit necessary.

 T. SUTINEN • PALM BEACH GARDENS, FL

Orangetini

1 ½ oz. Absolut vodka
Dash Martini & Rossi extra dry vermouth
Splash Hiram Walker triple sec
Orange peel for garnish

Stir gently and strain over ice. Garnish with the
orange peel.

Original Cosmopolitan

1 ½ oz. vodka
1 oz. Cointreau
1 oz. cranberry juice
¾ oz. fresh lime juice
Lemon twist for garnish

Shake over ice, and strain into a chilled martini
glass. Garnish with the lemon twist.

Original Martinez Cocktail

1 part Old Tom gin
1 part sweet vermouth
2 dashes simple syrup
Dash Angostura bitters
Dash maraschino cherry juice
Lemon slice to garnish

Shake with ice, and strain into a chilled martini glass. Serve on the rocks or straight up. Garnish with the lemon slice.

Original Sin Martini

1 oz. DeKuyper Apple Barrel schnapps
1 oz. vodka

Shake with ice, and strain into a chilled martini glass. Serve on the rocks or straight up.

The Original White Lady

2 oz. gin
1 oz. Cointreau
½ oz. fresh lemon juice

Shake with ice, and strain into a chilled martini glass.

Oyster Martini

2 ½ oz. Skyy vodka, chilled
3 freshly shucked oysters

Shake with ice, and serve over freshly shucked
oysters from the raw bar.

 EASTSIDE WEST • SAN FRANCISCO, CA

Ozzon Martini

2 ½ oz. Skyy vodka
Splash Romana Black sambuca
Olive for garnish

Stir with ice, and strain into a chilled martini
glass. Garnish with the olive.

 CLUB 36 • SAN FRANCISCO, CA

Paisley

2 oz. Bombay Sapphire gin
½ oz. dry vermouth
½ oz. single malt scotch whiskey
Twist for garnish

Shake with ice, and strain into a chilled martini
glass. Serve on the rocks or straight up. Garnish
with the twist.

Pall Mall Martini

1 ½ oz. Bombay Sapphire gin
½ oz. dry vermouth
½ oz. sweet vermouth
1 tsp. white crème de menthe
Dash Angostura bitters, optional

Stir ingredients with ice.

Palmetto Martini

1 ½ oz. rum
1 oz. sweet vermouth
2 dashes bitters
Lemon twist for garnish

Chill, strain, and serve in a chilled glass. Garnish with the lemon twist.

Panache Martini

2 ½ oz. Grey Goose vodka
¼ oz. Pernod
¼ oz. white crème de menthe
Whisper dry vermouth

 MERIDIEN HOTEL • BOSTON, MA

Paradigm Shift

"Entering an alternative martini dimension."

⅛ oz. Campari
1 oz. freshly squeezed Texas Ruby Red
   grapefruit juice
1 oz. fresh raspberry lemon-lime sour
2 oz. Rain vodka
¾ oz. Bombay Sapphire gin
Frozen grapefruit slice for garnish
Frozen raspberry for garnish

Start with an empty ice-cold martini mixing glass.
Lightly coat the mixing glass with Campari.
Dispose of excess. Fill the mixing glass with
ice. Squeeze Texas Ruby Red grapefruit into the
glass. Add fresh raspberry lemon-lime sour. Pour
Rain vodka and Bombay Sapphire gin into mixing glass. Cap and shake vigorously. Strain the
mixture into a frozen martini glass. Garnish with
the frozen grapefruit slice and frozen raspberry.

 OLIVER'S IN MAYFLOWER PARK HOTEL •
SEATTLE, WA

Paris Carver Martini

Lime wedge to rim
Sugar to rim
2 oz. Smirnoff vodka
Splash Romana Black sambuca
Lime for garnish

Run the lime wedge around the rim of a martini
glass, and coat with sugar. Chill, strain, and garnish with the lime.

Parisian Kiss Martini

2 oz. Smirnoff vodka
Splash Pernod
Juniper berries for garnish

Chill, strain, and sprinkle with juniper berries.

Parisian Martini

1 oz. Bombay Sapphire gin
1 oz. crème de cassis
1 oz. Martini & Rossi extra dry vermouth

Chill, and strain into a chilled martini glass.

Parisian Martini II

2 ½ oz. Tanqueray gin
Dash Pernod
Tomolive for garnish

Stir with ice, and strain into a chilled martini glass. Garnish with the Tomolive.

 COMPASS ROSE • SAN FRANCISCO, CA

Park Avenue Martini

1 ½ oz. gin
1 oz. pineapple juice
½ oz. sweet vermouth
2-3 drops of curaçao

Stir with ice, and strain into a chilled martini glass.

Park Place Martini

1 oz. Bombay Sapphire gin
1 oz. Chambord
Dash triple sec
Lemon zest for garnish

Shake with ice, and strain into a chilled martini glass. Serve on the rocks or straight up. Garnish with the lemon zest.

Parrot Head

1 oz. Malibu
1 oz. Midori melon liqueur
½ oz. pineapple juice
⅛ oz. grenadine

Shake with ice, and strain into a chilled martini glass. Serve on the rocks or straight up.

 GATSBY • BOCA RATON, FL

Pasha Martini

2 oz. Grey Goose
1 oz. Midori melon liqueur
½ to 1 oz. Chambord

Shake the first two ingredients rapidly over ice. Pour in Chambord. No garnish.

 JIM BACUS • PASHA • CHICAGO, IL

Passion Fruit Martini

2 oz. vodka
½ oz. Alizé
¼ oz. cranberry juice
¼ oz. Remy Martin VSOP

Shake with ice, and strain into a chilled martini glass. Serve on the rocks or straight up.

Passionfruit Blast Martini

2 oz. DeKuyper Sour Apple Pucker schnapps
2 oz. Stolichnaya Strasberi
1½ oz. pineapple juice
½ oz. DeKuyper Watermelon Pucker schnapps
Star fruit for garnish

Shake with ice, and strain into a chilled martini
glass. Garnish with the star fruit.

 DIANA AFONSO • MANHATTAN'S RESTAURANT •
MILFORD, MA

Patsy's Martini

1 ½ oz. Stolichnaya vodka
1 oz. champagne

 THE MARTINI CLUB • ATLANTA, GA

306

Peach Bellini-Tini

3 oz. Stolichnaya Peachik
1 ½ oz. DeKuyper Peachtree schnapps
1 oz. fresh peach puree
Champagne to top
Peach slice for garnish

Shake with ice, and strain into a chilled martini glass. Serve on the rocks or straight up. Top with champagne, and garnish with the peach slice.

 BACI GRILL • CROMWELL, CT

Peach Dream Martini

1 oz. Stolichnaya Peachik vodka
⅛ oz. DeKuyper Peachtree schnapps
⅛ oz. Malibu rum

Serve on the rocks, strained in a chilled "up" glass.

 ERIC SCHMIDT • CAFÉ WINBERIE • OAK PARK, IL

Peach Fuzz

2 oz. Stolichnaya Peachik vodka
¼ oz. Cointreau
¼ oz. orange juice
¼ oz. peach schnapps

Shake with ice, and strain into a chilled martini glass. Serve on the rocks or straight up.

 GATSBY • BOCA RATON, FL

Peach Martini

2 oz. Skyy vodka
¼ oz. peach schnapps

Shake with ice, and strain into a chilled martini glass. Serve on the rocks or straight up.

Peaches & Cream

1 ½ oz. Stolichnaya Peachik vodka
½ oz. Stolichnaya Vanil vodka
Peach slice for garnish

 CLUB XIX AT THE LODGE AT PEBBLE BEACH •
PEBBLE BEACH, CA

Peachie-Keen Martini

2 oz. Finlandia Arctic Cranberry vodka,
chilled
¼ oz. peach schnapps

Shake with ice, and strain into a chilled martini
glass.

Peachini Martini

2 cups fresh-skinned peaches
3 oz. vodka
Small scoop crushed ice

Blend till smooth.

 JILL STEVENS • TRABUCO CANYON, CA

Pear Martini

Sugar to rim
Dried orange rind to rim
2 oz. Grey Goose vodka
½ oz. Cointreau
½ oz. freshly squeezed lime juice

Rim a martini glass with sugar and the orange
rind. Shake with ice, and strain into the glass.

 THOMAS MASTRICOLA • 9 PARK • BOSTON, MA

Pear Martini II

2 oz. Stolichnaya vodka
½ oz. Perle de Brillet liqueur
Pear slice for garnish

Shake with ice, and serve in a chilled martini glass. Garnish with the pear slice.

Pearl Martini

2 oz. Absolut Mandrin vodka
½ oz. white cranberry juice
¼ oz. simple syrup
Lime slice for garnish

Shake well with ice. Garnish with the lime slice.

 THE SHORES RESTAURANT • LA JOLLA, CA

Pearsian Kat

1 ½ oz. Hiram Walker pear schnapps
1 oz. crème de cacao
1 oz. Stolichnaya Vanil vodka
Chocolate syrup for garnish

Shake with ice, and strain into a martini glass. Garnish with the drizzle of chocolate syrup.

Peatini

1 oz. gin
Splash vermouth
1 Texas-sized black-eyed pea

Shake with crushed ice, and strain into a glass.
Garnish with the black-eyed pea.

 MARIANNE STEVENS • EMAILED TO OUR BLOG,
WWW.BARTENDERMAGAZINE.WORDPRESS.COM

Peggy Martini

1 ½ oz. Gordon's Special Dry London gin
¾ oz. Martini & Rossi extra dry vermouth
¼ oz. Dubonnet
¼ oz. Pernod

Shake with ice, and strain into a chilled martini
glass. Serve on the rocks or straight up.

Peppar Martini

2 oz. Absolut Peppar vodka
¼ oz. Cinzano dry vermouth
Jalapeño-stuffed olive for garnish

Shake with ice, and strain into a chilled martini
glass. Serve on the rocks or straight up. Garnish
with the olive.

Peppermint Martini

2 oz. vodka
½ oz. Rumple Minze

Shake with ice, and strain into a chilled martini glass. Serve on the rocks or straight up.

Peppermint Patty Martini

2 ½ oz. Grey Goose vodka
½ oz. peppermint schnapps
½ oz. white crème de cacao
2 junior mints for garnish

Shake with ice, and strain into a chilled martini glass. Garnish with the two Junior Mints on a pick.

 MICHAEL MIKA OF HARVEY'S • BOSTON, MA

Peppertini

1 ½ oz. Stolichnaya Pertsovka vodka
½ oz. dry vermouth
Olive for garnish

Mix vodka and dry vermouth in a cocktail shaker over ice, stir, and strain. Garnish with the olive.

The "Perfect" Martini

2 oz. Bombay Sapphire gin
Eye-dropper of dry vermouth
Jumbo shrimp for garnish
Cocktail sauce for garnish

Shake with ice, and strain into a chilled martini
glass. Serve on the rocks or straight up. Garnish
with the jumbo shrimp and cocktail sauce.

 SHULA'S NO NAME LOUNGE • MULTIPLE
LOCATIONS IN FLORIDA

Perfect Martini

1 ¾ oz. Bombay Sapphire gin
¼ oz. Martini & Rossi extra dry vermouth
¼ oz. Martini & Rossi Rosso sweet vermouth
Lemon twist for garnish

Blend and stir. Garnish with the lemon twist.

Perfect Martini II

2 oz. Bombay Sapphire gin
1 oz. French vermouth
1 oz. Italian vermouth
Dash bitters
Lemon twist for garnish

Shake with ice, and strain into a chilled martini glass. Garnish with the lemon twist.

 ADAPTED FROM NASSAU GUN CLUB RECIPE

Perfect Pair

1 ½ oz. Grey Goose vodka
½ oz. fresh lemon juice
½ oz. pear eau de vie
½ oz. simple syrup
Splash orange juice

Shake with ice, and strain into a chilled martini glass. Serve on the rocks or straight up.

 MARCO DIANYSOS • ABSINTHE •
SAN FRANCISCO, CA

Perfect Royal Martini

¾ oz. dry gin
¾ oz. dry vermouth
¾ oz. sweet vermouth
¼ oz. Pernod
Green cherry for garnish

Shake with ice, and strain into a chilled martini glass. Serve on the rocks or straight up. Garnish with the cherry.

Perfection Martini

1 ½ oz. Bombay Sapphire gin
Dash Martini & Rossi Rosso sweet vermouth
Lemon twist or olives for garnish (optional)

Stir with ice, and strain into a chilled martini glass. Serve straight up or on the rocks. Garnish with the lemon twist or olives.

Perfection Martini II

1 ¾ oz. dry gin
½ oz. orange juice
½ oz. sweet vermouth

Shake with ice, and strain into a chilled martini glass. Serve on the rocks or straight up.

Pernod Martini

2 oz. dry gin
½ oz. dry vermouth
2 dashes Pernod

Shake with ice, and strain into a chilled martini glass. Serve on the rocks or straight up.

Phantom Martini

2 oz. Ketel One vodka
¼ oz. Johnny Walker Black Label
Jumbo black olive for garnish

Shake with ice, and strain into a chilled martini glass. Serve on the rocks or straight up.

 MORTON'S "MARTINI CLUB" • SAN ANTONIO, TX

Piccadilly Cocktail Martini

1 ½ oz. Beefeater gin
¾ oz. Martini & Rossi extra dry vermouth
¼ tsp. grenadine
¼ tsp. Pernod or other anise-flavored liqueur

Stir with ice, and strain into a chilled glass.

Pickled Pepper Martini

2 oz. Absolut Peppar vodka
Splash pickle juice
Dill pickle slice for garnish

Shake with ice, and strain into a chilled martini
glass. Garnish with a pickle slice.

 POMONA, CA

Piña Colada Martini

1 part Cruzan coconut rum
1 part Cruzan pineapple rum
Splash pineapple juice

Stir with ice, and strain into a martini glass.

Pink Diamond Martini

2 oz. pineapple juice
1 oz. Finlandia Arctic Cranberry vodka
1 oz. Finlandia Classic vodka
1 oz. peach schnapps
Maraschino cherry or rose petals for garnish

Stir gently with ice, and strain into a glass. Garnish
with the maraschino cherry or rose petals.

Pink Martini

1 ½ oz. Absolut vodka
½ oz. cranberry juice
Dash dry vermouth
Lime squeeze

Shake the first three ingredients with ice, and strain into a chilled martini glass. Serve on the rocks or straight up. Top with a lime squeeze.

 RANDY WICKSTROM • RAINFOREST •
BEACH PARK, IL

Pink Martini Twist

2 ½ oz. Absolut Kurant vodka
¼ oz. Chambord

 PORTLAND'S BEST • PORTLAND, OR

Pink Poodle Martini

¾ oz. Stolichnaya vodka
¼ oz. Chambord
¼ oz. white crème de cacao
Fresh raspberry for garnish

Stir over ice, and strain into a chilled martini glass. Garnish with the fresh raspberry.

 SCOTT DISTEFANO • SUSIE'S BAR • CALISTOGA, CA

Pink Rose

2 oz. Skyy vodka
1 oz. DeKuyper Peachtree schnapps
¼ oz. cranberry juice

Shake with ice, and strain into a chilled martini glass. Serve on the rocks or straight up.

Pink Stingray Martini

2 ½ oz. Finlandia Arctic Cranberry vodka
¼ oz. white crème de cacao

Shake with ice, and strain into a chilled martini glass. Serve on the rocks or straight up.

Pink Swan Cocktail

Sugar to rim
2 oz. Bacardi Añejo rum
¼ oz. Cointreau
¼ oz. sweet and sour mix
2 maraschino cherries for garnish
Lime circle for garnish
Short straws

Rim a martini glass with sugar. Blend with ice, and serve in the glass. Garnish with the cherries and lime circle; offer short straws.

 HOTEL BEL-AIR • LOS ANGELES, CA

Pinsk Peach

2 oz. Stolichnaya Peachik vodka
½ oz. Campari

Shake with ice, and strain into a chilled martini glass. Serve straight up.

Pitbull in the Sky

2 oz. Skyy vodka
¼ oz. grapefruit juice
Twist for garnish

Shake; do not stir. Serve straight up in an over-sized chilled stem. Garnish with the twist.

Platini

3 oz. Tarantula Plata
Splash Martini & Rossi extra dry vermouth
Splash Tabasco
1 small jalapeño pepper for garnish

Shake with ice, and strain into a chilled martini
glass. Garnish with the jalapeño pepper.

Plaza Martini

1 ½ oz. Bombay Sapphire gin
1 ½ oz. Martini & Rossi extra dry vermouth
Lemon twist or olives for garnish

Stir with ice, and strain into a cocktail glass.
Serve straight up or on the rocks. Garnish with
the lemon twist or olives.

Plaza Martini II

1 oz. Bombay Sapphire gin
1 oz. Martini & Rossi extra dry vermouth
1 oz. Martini & Rossi Rosso sweet vermouth
Splash pineapple juice

Shake with ice, and strain into a chilled martini
glass. Serve on the rocks or straight up.

Plymouth Cocktail Martini

2 ½ oz. dry gin
2 dashes orange bitters

Poet's Dream Martini

1 oz. Bombay Sapphire gin
¾ oz. Benedictine
¾ oz. Martini & Rossi extra dry vermouth
Lemon twist for garnish

Shake with ice, and strain into a chilled martini
glass. Serve on the rocks or straight up.

Poinsettia Martini

1 ½ oz. Absolut vodka
¼ oz. Chambord
¼ oz. pineapple juice

Shake with ice, and strain into a martini glass.

 LINDA BETT • LONGNECKERS SALOON •
HOUSTON, TX

Polo Cocktail Martini

1 ½ oz. gin
¾ oz. fresh orange juice
½ oz. fresh lemon juice

Shake with ice, and strain into a chilled glass.

Polo Martini

1 ½ oz. Perrier-Jouet champagne
1 ½ oz. Sobieski vodka
Dash Peychaud bitters
Olive for garnish
Twist for garnish

Serve straight up in a martini glass. Garnish with
the olive and the twist on the side.

 WINDSOR COURT HOTEL • NEW ORLEANS, LA

Polo Martini Club

1 oz. Bombay Sapphire gin
½ oz. Martini & Rossi extra dry vermouth
⅓ oz. Martini & Rossi Rosso sweet vermouth
¼ oz. lime juice

Shake with ice, and strain into a chilled martini
glass. Serve on the rocks or straight up.

Polynesian Martini

Confectioner's sugar to rim
1 ½ oz. Smirnoff vodka
¾ oz. cherry-flavored brandy
Splash lime juice

Rim glass with the sugar. Chill, and strain into
the martini glass.

Pom Pom Martini

1 ½ oz. dry vermouth
¾ oz. dry gin
2 dashes orange bitters

Shake with ice, and strain into a chilled martini
glass. Serve on the rocks or straight up.

Pom Sidecar

1 oz. Hennessy VS
1 oz. simple syrup
¾ oz. fresh lemon juice
½ oz. Grand Marnier
½ oz. pomegranate concentrate
1 egg white, organic
Dash orange bitters
Thyme for garnish

Shake well over ice, and strain into a martini glass. Garnish with the thyme.

Pomegranate Martini

2 oz. pomegranate juice
2 oz. vodka
½ oz. Cointreau
Splash lime juice

Shake with ice, and strain into a martini glass.

Poo'Tini

2 ½ oz. Belvedere vodka
½ oz. honey

Shake with ice, and strain into a chilled martini glass. Serve on the rocks or straight up.

Presidente Martini

1 ½ oz. light rum
½ oz. dry vermouth
1 tsp. triple sec
1-2 dashes grenadine
Lemon twist for garnish

Shake with cracked ice, and strain into a chilled glass. Garnish with the lemon twist.

Presidente Martini II

1 ½ oz. Bacardi rum
¾ oz. Martini & Rossi Rosso sweet vermouth
¼ oz. Martini & Rossi extra dry vermouth
Dash grenadine
Maraschino cherry for garnish

Shake with cracked ice, and strain into a chilled glass. Garnish with the maraschino cherry.

Pressini

1 oz. Pernod
2 oz. fresh chilled espresso
3 white coffee beans for garnish

In a chilled martini glass, pour Pernod and fill with chilled espresso. Garnish with white coffee beans.

Prince's Grin

2 oz. Tanqueray gin
1 oz. apple juice
1 oz. apricot nectar
½ tsp. fresh lemon juice

Shake ingredients with ice, and strain into a chilled glass.

Prince's Smile Martini

2 oz. Tanqueray gin
1 oz. apple brandy
1 oz. apricot brandy
½ tsp. fresh lemon juice

Shake ingredients with ice, and strain into a chilled glass.

Princess Mary

⅓ part Cork dry gin
⅓ part crème de cacao
⅓ part fresh cream

Shake, and strain into a chilled martini glass.

Princeton Martini

1 ½ oz. dry gin
1 oz. port
2 dashes orange bitters
Lemon twist for garnish

Shake with ice, and strain into a chilled martini glass. Serve on the rocks or straight up. Garnish with the lemon twist.

Provincetown-Tini

Stolichnaya Ohranj vodka
Splash Finlandia Arctic Cranberry vodka

 THE DINER ON SYCAMORE • CINCINNATI, OH

Psychedelic Martini

2 oz. Beefeater gin
½ oz. orange juice
½ oz. pineapple juice
¼ oz. Martini & Rossi extra dry vermouth
¼ oz. Martini & Rossi Rosso sweet vermouth
Dash anisette

Shake with ice, and strain into a chilled martini glass. Serve on the rocks or straight up.

Puckered Up Apple Kiss

2 ½ oz. DeKuyper Sour Apple Pucker
   schnapps
½ oz. vodka, chilled

Shake with ice, and strain into a chilled martini glass.

Pump Martini

Olives, lemon twist, or onions
Benedictine to marinate
1 ½ oz. vodka
Splash dry vermouth

In one mixing glass, marinate the olives, lemon twist, or onions in Benedictine. In a second mixing glass combine vodka, vermouth, and several ice cubes. Stir, and strain into a chilled martini glass. Garnish with the marinated olives, lemon twist, or onions.

 THE PUMP ROOM • CHICAGO, IL

Punt e Mes Negroni

¾ oz. Boodles gin
¾ oz. Martini & Rossi Rosso sweet vermouth
¾ oz. Punt e Mes vermouth
Twist lemon peel for garnish

Shake with ice, and strain into a chilled martini glass. Serve on the rocks or straight up. Garnish with the twist.

Pure Martini

2 oz. Bombay Sapphire gin
1 tsp. Noilly Prat dry vermouth
2 Spanish cocktail olives for garnish

In a shaker half-filled with ice, combine gin and vermouth. Shake well, and strain into a chilled martini glass. Garnish with olives skewered on a pick.

 THE RITZ-CARLTON BAR AT THE RITZ CARLTON
• SAN FRANCISCO, CA

Pure Precipitation Martini

2 oz. Rain vodka, chilled
Orange slice for garnish

Shake with ice, and strain into a martini glass. Garnish with the orange slice.

Puritan Martini

1 ¾ oz. Bombay Sapphire gin
½ oz. Martini & Rossi extra dry vermouth
¼ oz. yellow Chartreuse
Dash orange bitters

Purple Haze Martini

2 ½ oz. Sobieski vodka
2 oz. sweet and sour
½ oz. raspberry liqueur or Chambord
Splash 7-Up

Make in a pint glass filled with ice. Shake, and
serve with strainer and martini glass.

 ROBERT LEHMANN, OFFICE MANAGER •
THE BROADWAY GRILL • SEATTLE, WA

Purple Haze Martini II

½ oz. Chambord
½ oz. Sobieski vodka
Dash triple sec
Splash lime juice
Splash soda water

Shake with ice, and strain into a chilled martini
glass. Serve on the rocks or straight up.

Purple Hooter Martini

1 oz. Sobieski vodka
½ oz. Chambord
½ oz. lemon-lime soda
½ oz sour mix

Shake with ice, and strain into a chilled martini
glass. Serve on the rocks or straight up.

Purple Mask

1 ½ oz. Smirnoff vodka
1 oz. grape juice
Splash white crème de cacao

Stir with ice, and strain into a chilled martini
glass.

Purple People Eater

2 oz. Bacardi Limón rum
2 oz. cranberry juice
⅛ oz. blue curaçao
⅛ oz. Martini & Rossi extra dry vermouth

Shake with ice, and strain into a chilled martini
glass.

Purple Rain Martini

1 part Chambord, chilled
1 part Rain vodka, chilled
Lime twist for garnish

Shake with ice, and strain into a martini glass.
Garnish with the lime twist.

 RAIN VODKA

Purpletini

2 oz. Absolut Kurant vodka
½ oz. Chambord
½ oz. triple sec
Lemon twist for garnish

Shake with ice, and strain into a chilled martini
glass. Serve on the rocks or straight up. Garnish
with the lemon twist.

 MARK PROUTY • GROUND ROUND •
FRAMINGHAM, MA

The "Q" Martini

2 oz. Smirnoff vodka
Splash blue curaçao
Dash lime juice
Lemon twist for garnish

Chill, and strain into a glass. Garnish with the lemon twist.

Queen Elizabeth Martini

1 ½ oz. Bombay Sapphire gin
Dash Martini & Rossi extra dry vermouth
Splash Benedictine
Lemon twist or olives for garnish

Stir with ice, and strain into a glass. Serve straight up or on the rocks. Garnish with the lemon twist or olives.

Queenie-Tini

2 oz. Absolut Kurant vodka
¼ oz. Chambord
¼ oz. champagne

Shake with ice, and strain into a chilled martini glass. Serve on the rocks or straight up.

The "Quigg" Martini

1 ½ oz. Midori melon liqueur
1 oz. Jameson Irish whiskey
Splash peach schnapps
Splash sour mix
Maraschino cherry for garnish

Shake with ice, and strain into a chilled martini glass with a maraschino cherry on the bottom.

 HEATH POLKINGHORN • MANHATTAN, KS

R & R Martini

1 ½ oz. Gordon's vodka
Dash aquavit

R.A.C.

2 oz. Cork dry gin
¼ oz. dry vermouth
Dash grenadine
Dash orange bitters
1 maraschino cherry for garnish
Orange twist for garnish

Mix, and garnish with the maraschino cherry and orange twist.

Radartini

2 oz. Smirnoff vodka
1 oz. tomato juice
Olive for garnish

Shake with ice, and strain into a chilled martini glass. Serve on the rocks or straight up. Garnish with the olive.

 THE WINDSOCK BAR & GRILL • SAN DIEGO, CA

Ragazzi Che Martini

2 oz. Belvedere vodka
¼ oz. apricot brandy
¼ oz. Godiva original liqueur
¼ oz. grapefruit juice

Shake with ice, and strain into a chilled martini glass. Serve on the rocks or straight up.

 MAD 28 • NEW YORK, NY

Raidme Martini

1 ¾ oz. dry gin
½ oz. Pernod
¼ oz. Campari

Shake with ice, and strain into a chilled martini glass. Serve on the rocks or straight up.

Rain Love Martini

1 oz. Rain vodka
½ oz. white crème de cacao
¼ oz. Chambord

Chill, and serve in a classic martini glass.

 MARCOVALDO DIONYSAS, BARTENDER • ABSINTHE
BAR & RESTAURANT • SAN FRANCISCO, CA

Rainforest Martini

Orange wedge
Pineapple wedge (plus extra for garnish)
½ oz. banana liqueur
½ oz. Midori melon liqueur
1 oz. Patrón Silver tequila
½ oz. blue curaçao
½ oz Malibu rum
Splash pineapple juice and sour mix
Maraschino cherry for garnish

Muddle the orange wedge, the pineapple wedge,
banana liqueur, and Midori. Add ice and shake
vigorously. Add remaining ingredients. Shake
and strain into a chilled martini glass. Garnish
with the pineapple wedge and maraschino cherry.

 SUE SANTOS • UNO CHICAGO BAR & GRILL
• PLYMOUTH, MA

Rainier Martini

12 sour cherries
1 oz. Belvedere vodka
1 Calvados-marinated Bing cherry for
  garnish

Combine sour cherries with vodka, and let stand
24 hours. Stir well with ice, and strain into an ice-
cold martini glass. Garnish with the Calvados-
marinated Bing cherry.

 GARDEN COURT AT THE FOUR SEASONS OLYMPIC
HOTEL • SEATTLE, WA

Ranch-style Martini

2 oz. vodka or gin
¼ oz. Patrón Silver tequila
Pickled olive for garnish

Shake with ice, and strain into a chilled martini
glass. Serve on the rocks or straight up.

 SHERATON SEATTLE • SEATTLE, WA

Rasbertini

2 oz. Stolichnaya Razberi vodka
¼ oz. Stolichnaya Ohranj vodka
Orange slice for garnish

Shake with ice, and strain into a chilled martini glass. Serve on the rocks or straight up. Garnish with the orange slice.

 RENAISSANCE ATLANTA HOTEL • ATLANTA, GA

Raschocolate Martini

2 oz. cranberry juice
1 ½ oz. Smirnoff vodka
1 oz. white crème de cacao
Dash raspberry liqueur

Chill, and strain into a chilled martini glass.

Raspberry Chocolate Martini

1 ½ oz. Chambord
1 ½ oz. white crème de cacao
Raspberry for garnish

Shake with ice, and strain into a glass. Serve on the rocks or straight up. Garnish with the raspberry.

 JOSEPH VUCKOVIC • EMAILED TO OUR BLOG,
WWW.BARTENDERMAGAZINE.WORDPRESS.COM

Raspberry Martini

1 ½ oz. gin or vodka
½ oz. Chambord
Lemon twist or olive for garnish

Pour over ice. Garnish with the lemon twist or olive.

Raspberry Martini II

2 oz. Smirnoff vodka
Splash raspberry liqueur
Fresh raspberries as garnish

Stir with ice, and strain into a glass. Garnish with fresh raspberries.

Raspberry Truffle

Cocoa powder to rim
1 ½ oz. vodka
½ oz. Baileys Irish cream
½ oz. Chambord
½ oz. Kahlúa
Mist Martini & Rossi extra dry vermouth
Chocolate stick for garnish
Raspberry for garnish

Rim a martini glass with cocoa powder. Shake with ice, and strain into the chilled glass. Garnish with the chocolate stick and raspberry.

Raspberry Twist Martini

1 ½ oz. Ketel One vodka
1 oz. Bonny Doon Framboise infusion
   (local product)
¼ oz. Chambord
Fresh raspberries for garnish

 POLO LOUNGE • WINDSOR COURT HOTEL •
NEW ORLEANS, LA

Raspberry Vodka Martini

2 oz. Stolichnaya Razberi vodka
Splash Chambord liqueur
Lime twist for garnish

Shake with ice, and strain into a chilled martini
glass. Garnish with the lime twist.

 JASON WINGERTER • PERONI WATERFRONT
RESTAURANT

Rattlesnake Martini

2 oz. Stolichnaya Cristall vodka
¼ oz. Chambord
2 splashes cranberry juice
Splash pineapple juice
Squeeze lemon and lime
Twist for garnish

Shake, and serve straight up. Garnish with the twist.

 BOBBY CARROLL • RATTLESNAKE BAR & GRILL •
BOSTON, MA

Razzle Dazzle

1 oz. Stolichnaya Razberi vodka
Splash Chambord
Lemon twist for garnish

Shake with ice, and strain into a chilled martini glass. Serve on the rocks or straight up. Garnish with the lemon twist.

 PEGGY HOWELL • COTATI YACHT CLUB &
SALOON • COTATI, CA

Real Gordon's Martini

2 ½ oz. Gordon's vodka
⅛ oz. dry vermouth
Lemon twist for garnish

Shake with ice, and strain into a chilled martini glass. Serve on the rocks or straight up.

Re-Bar Red

2 oz. Campari
Juice 2 lemon wedges
Juice 2 lime wedges
Splash 7-Up

Shake with ice, and strain into a chilled martini glass. Serve on the rocks or straight up.

Red Apple Martini

¾ oz. dry gin
¾ oz. sweet vermouth
½ oz. apple brandy
½ oz. grenadine

Shake with ice, and strain into a chilled martini glass. Serve on the rocks or straight up.

Red Gin-Gin Martini

2 oz. gin
½ oz. sloe gin
⅛ oz. dry vermouth
Spiral orange twist for garnish

Stir with ice, and strain into a chilled martini glass. Garnish with the spiral orange twist.

 THE MANDARIN • SAN FRANCISCO, CA

Red Martini

2 oz. Beefeater gin
$1/10$ oz. dry vermouth
Dash Campari
Lemon wedge for garnish

Shake over ice, and strain into a chilled martini glass. Garnish with the lemon.

Red Martini II

1 ½ oz. gin
½ oz. sloe gin
Dash grenadine

Shake with ice, and strain into a chilled martini glass. Serve on the rocks or straight up.

Red Nut

Stolichnaya vodka
Splash Frangelico

Shake with ice, and strain into a chilled martini
glass. Serve on the rocks or straight up.

 HOTEL SAN REMO • LAS VEGAS, NV

Red Passion Martini

1 ½ oz. Alizé
½ oz. Campari
Orange peel for garnish

Stir well, and serve in a martini glass. Garnish
with the orange peel.

Red Rim Martini

Sweet vermouth to rim
Red sugar to rim
1 ½ oz. raspberry-white grape juice
1 oz. Gordon's vodka
Blackberry for garnish

Rim a glass with sweet vermouth. Dip rim in red
sugar. Garnish with the blackberry.

Red Room Martini

2 oz. Stolichnaya Razberi vodka
1 oz. Alizé Red Passion
Splash sour mix
Twist for garnish

Shake with ice, and strain into a glass. Garnish
with the twist.

Red Royal Martini

2 oz. Crown Royal whiskey
½ oz. amaretto

Shake with ice, and strain into a chilled martini
glass. Serve on the rocks or straight up.

 PORTLAND'S BEST • PORTLAND, OR

Red-hot Martini

2 oz. vodka
½ oz. cinnamon schnapps
¼ oz. Romana Black sambuca
Red Hots for garnish

Shake with ice, and strain into a chilled martini
glass. Serve on the rocks or straight up. Garnish
with the Red Hots.

Redwood Room Martini

3 oz. Grey Goose vodka
3 olives, one stuffed with Gorgonzola
    cheese for garnish
1 eye drop vermouth

 JOE WATTS • THE CLIFT HOTEL'S REDWOOD ROOM
    • SAN FRANCISCO, CA

Reebok Martini

2 ½ oz. Skyy vodka
½ oz. Martini & Rossi extra dry vermouth
½ oz. peach schnapps
Lemon twist soaked in Grand Marnier for
    garnish

Shake with ice, and strain into a chilled martini
glass. Serve on the rocks or straight up. Garnish
with the lemon twist.

 REEBOK SPORTS CLUB • NEW YORK, NY

Reform Cocktail Martini

1 ½ oz. dry sherry
¾ oz. dry vermouth
Dash orange bitters
Maraschino cherry for garnish

Stir with ice, and strain into a chilled glass.
Garnish with the maraschino cherry.

Rendezvous Martini

1 ½ oz. dry gin
½ oz. kirschwasser
¼ oz. Campari
Lemon twist for garnish

Shake with ice, and strain into a chilled martini
glass. Serve on the rocks or straight up. Garnish
with the lemon twist.

Richmond Martini

1 ¾ oz. dry gin
¾ oz. Lillet
Lemon twist for garnish

Shake with ice, and strain into a chilled martini
glass. Serve on the rocks or straight up. Garnish
with the lemon twist.

Rising Sun Martini

2 oz. Skyy vodka
Mist Grand Marnier
Orange twist for garnish

Shake, do not stir. Serve up in an oversized chilled martini glass. Garnish with the orange twist.

Robin's Nest

1 ½ oz. Smirnoff vodka
1 oz. cranberry juice
Splash white crème de cacao

Chill, and strain into a martini glass.

Robyn's Blue Bomber

2 oz. Beefeater gin
1 drop dry vermouth
¼ oz. blue curaçao

Shake with ice, and strain into a chilled martini glass.

 ROBYN SUCHOWSKI • ELIZABETH, NJ

Rockefeller

2 oz. Hennessy VS
½ oz. Stolichnaya vodka
½ oz. champagne, chilled
Lemon twist for garnish

Coat the inside of a chilled martini glass with
Hennessy, and discard excess. Mix the vodka in
a mixing tin, and stir. Add cold champagne just
before straining into a glass. Garnish with the
lemon twist.

Rolls Royce Martini

2 oz. dry gin
1 oz. sweet vermouth
½ oz. Benedictine
½ oz. dry vermouth

Shake with ice, and strain into a glass.

Roma Martini

1 ½ oz. dry gin
½ oz. dry vermouth
½ oz. sweet vermouth
3 fresh strawberries

Mix all ingredients, including the strawberries.
Serve on the rocks or straight up in a chilled
martini glass.

Rosa Martini

1 ½ oz. Bombay Sapphire gin
¼ oz. Hiram Walker Cherry brandy
¼ oz. Martini & Rossi extra dry vermouth
Lemon twist or olives for garnish

Stir in a cocktail glass. Strain, and serve straight
up or on the rocks. Garnish with the lemon twist
or olives.

Rosalin Russell Martini

1 ½ oz. Bombay Sapphire gin
Dash aquavit
Lemon twist or olives for garnish

Shake with ice, and strain into glass. Serve on
the rocks or straight up. Garnish with the lemon
twist or olives.

Rose du Boy

1 ½ oz. dry gin
½ oz. dry vermouth
¼ oz. cherry-flavored brandy
¼ oz. kirschwasser

Shake with ice, and strain into a chilled martini
glass. Serve on the rocks or straight up.

Rose Kennedy Martini

3 oz. lemonade (preferably fresh squeezed)
1 ½ oz. vodka
1 oz. peach schnapps
Splash cranberry juice
Lime wedge for garnish

Fill a blender with ice; add the first four ingredients. Blend, and pour into a glass. Garnish with the lime wedge.

 PATRICK FORD • SMITH & WOLLENSKY'S •
NEW YORK, NY

Rose Marie Martini

1 ¼ oz. dry gin
½ oz. dry vermouth
¼ oz. Armagnac
¼ oz. Campari
¼ oz. cherry-flavored brandy

Shake with ice, and strain into a chilled martini glass. Serve on the rocks or straight up.

Rose Petal

2 oz. Belvedere vodka
½ oz. Grand Marnier
½ oz. Martini & Rossi extra dry vermouth
Rose petals for garnish

Shake with ice, and strain into a chilled martini glass. Garnish with rose petals.

 IGGY'S • CHICAGO, IL

Roselyn Martini

2 ½ oz. Bombay Sapphire gin
¼ oz. Martini & Rossi extra dry vermouth
⅛ oz. Rose's grenadine
Lemon twist or olives for garnish

Stir with ice, and strain into a glass. Serve straight up or on the rocks. Garnish with the lemon twist or olives.

Rose's Martini

1 ½ oz. Absolut vodka
Splash Chambord
Splash Rose's Lime Juice
Lime wedge for garnish

Mix in a shaker glass with ice, and strain into a
martini glass. Garnish with the lime wedge.

 DONNA ELDRIDGE, BAR MANAGER • SPUDS
RESTAURANT & PUB • DANVERS, MA

Royal Cocktail Martini

1 ¾ oz. dry gin
¾ oz. Dubonnet
Dash Angostura bitters
Dash orange bitters

Shake with ice, and strain into a chilled martini
glass. Serve on the rocks or straight up.

Royal Devil

2 oz. Stolichnaya Razberi vodka
½ oz. Blackhaus liqueur
½ oz. Chambord

Serve chilled and straight up.

Royal Romance

1 ½ oz. Cork dry gin
½ oz. passion fruit juice
¼ oz. Grand Marnier
Dash sugar syrup

Shake with ice, and strain into a chilled martini glass. Serve on the rocks or straight up.

Royal Wedding Martini

Tanqueray gin or Stolichnaya vodka
Dash Chivas Regal

Handsomely marry Tanqueray gin or Stolichnaya vodka to a dash of Chivas Regal.

 OLIVER'S IN MAYFLOWER PARK HOTEL
• SEATTLE, WA

Ruby Slipper Martini

2 oz. Bombay Sapphire gin
¼ oz. Grand Marnier
1 or 2 splashes grenadine
Dash peppermint schnapps
Mint leaf for garnish

Shake with ice, and strain into a chilled martini glass. Garnish with the mint leaf (set it on the edge of the drink and let it stick out).

Rum Martini

2 oz. light rum
¼ oz. French vermouth
Lemon twist for garnish

Shake with ice, and strain into a chilled martini glass. Serve on the rocks or straight up. Garnish with the lemon twist.

Runyons Martini

3 oz. Stolichnaya Ohranj vodka
Dash dry vermouth
Orange slice for garnish

Stir with ice, and strain into a chilled martini glass. Serve straight up. Garnish with the orange slice.

Ruski Limonnade

1 oz. Stolichnaya Limonnaya vodka
Splash simple syrup
Lemon twist for garnish

Shake with ice, and strain into a chilled martini glass. Serve on the rocks or straight up. Garnish with the lemon twist.

 PEGGY HOWELL • COTATI YACHT CLUB & SALOON • COTATI, CA

Russian Brushfire

2 ½ oz. Stolichnaya vodka
Bloody Mary mix
⅛ oz. Tabasco sauce
1 small jalapeño pepper for garnish

Mix vodka and small portion of Bloody Mary mix with ice (enough to make drink red in color). Shake, and strain into a chilled martini glass. Garnish with the Tabasco and pepper.

Russian Delight Martini

2 ½ oz. Stolichnaya Vanil vodka
¼ oz. Disaronno amaretto

Shake with ice, and strain into a chilled martini glass. Serve on the rocks or straight up.

Russian Malted Martini

2 oz. Stolichnaya vodka
¼ oz. Lagavulin (or comparable single malt scotch)
Twist for garnish

Russian Martini

¾ oz. gin
¾ oz. Stolichnaya vodka
¾ oz. white crème de cacao

Stir with ice, and strain into a chilled martini glass.

Russian Martini II

1 ½ oz. Stolichnaya Ohranj vodka
½ oz. champagne
Orange zest for garnish

 MARTINI'S • NEW YORK, NY

Russian Tiramisu

2 oz. Kahlúa
1 oz. Stolichnaya Vanil vodka

Shake with ice, and strain into a chilled martini glass. Serve on the rocks or straight up.

Saigon Martini

2 oz. Hennessy cognac
1 oz. Cointreau
1 oz. Zen Green Tea liqueur
2 dashes Rose's Lime Juice
Lime wedge for garnish

Shake with ice, and strain into a chilled cocktail glass. Garnish with the lime wedge.

 LISA ANN HOANG • MO MONG RESTAURANT • HOUSTON, TX

Sake Martini

2 oz. Stolichnaya Ohranj vodka
¼ oz. dry sake
Cucumber slice for garnish

Shake with ice, and strain into a chilled martini glass. Serve on the rocks or straight up. Garnish with the cucumber slice.

Sake'Politan

2 oz. premium cold sake
1 oz. Cointreau
¾ oz. cranberry juice
¼ oz. lime juice

Shake with ice, and fine strain into a chilled martini glass.

Sakitini Martini

1 ½ oz. Bombay Sapphire gin
Dash sake
Lemon twist or olives for garnish

Shake or stir, strain, and serve straight up or on the rocks in a cocktail glass. Garnish with the lemon twist or olives.

Sakitini Martini II

1 ½ oz. Smirnoff vodka at room temperature
2 ½ oz. hot sake
Pickled ginger for garnish
Dollop wasabi for garnish

Top vodka with sake. Garnish with the pickled ginger and wasabi.

Salome Martini

1 oz. dry gin
¾ oz. dry vermouth
¾ oz. Dubonnet

Shake with ice, and strain into a chilled martini glass. Serve on the rocks or straight up.

Salt 'N' Pepper

Salt to rim
2 ½ oz. Absolut Peppar vodka
Cocktail onions for garnish

Rim a glass with salt. Serve in a chilled glass.
Garnish with the onions.

 CECILIA'S • BRECKENRIDGE, CO

Sam I Am Martini

3 oz. cranberry juice
1 ¼ oz. Absolut Citron vodka
¼ oz. amaretto
Lemon twist for garnish

Shake with ice, and strain into a martini glass.
Serve straight up. Garnish with the lemon twist.

 SAMBONN LEK, HEAD BARTENDER • RENAISSANCE
MAYFLOWER HOTEL • WASHINGTON, DC

San Francisco Cocktail Martini

¾ oz. dry vermouth
¾ oz. sloe gin
¾ oz. sweet vermouth
Dash Angostura bitters
Dash orange bitters
Maraschino cherry for garnish

Shake with ice, and strain into a chilled glass.
Garnish with the maraschino cherry.

San Martin Martini

¾ oz. dry gin
¾ oz. dry vermouth
¾ oz. sweet vermouth
¼ oz. anisette
Dash bitters

Sapphire Martini

2 ½ oz. Bombay Sapphire gin
⅛ oz. Cinzano vermouth
Olive for garnish

Shake with ice, and strain into a chilled martini
glass. Serve on the rocks or straight up. Garnish
with the olive.

Sapphire Martini II

2 ½ oz. Bombay Sapphire gin
Pearl onions for garnish

Shake with ice, and strain into a chilled martini
glass. Serve on the rocks or straight up. Garnish
with the pearl onions.

 POLO LOUNGE • WINDSOR COURT HOTEL • NEW
ORLEANS, LA

Saratoga Martini

1 ½ oz. Smirnoff vodka
2 dashes Angostura bitters
2 dashes grenadine
Splash soda water
Pineapple wedge for garnish

Shake with ice, and strain into a chilled martini
glass. Serve on the rocks or straight up. Garnish
with the pineapple wedge.

Sargasso Martini

2 oz. Skyy vodka
¼ oz. blue curaçao
¼ oz. Midori melon liqueur
Lime twist for garnish

Sassy Jo

2 ½ oz. Bombay Sapphire gin
1 ½ oz. orange juice
¼ oz. dry vermouth
¼ oz. sweet vermouth
3 drops bitters

 BRASSERIE JO • CHICAGO, IL

Satan's Whiskers

½ oz. dry vermouth
½ oz. gin
½ oz. orange juice
¼ oz. Grand Marnier
¼ oz. sweet vermouth
Dash orange bitters or orange peel twists
Maraschino cherry for garnish
Orange slice for garnish

Shake with ice, and strain into a cocktail
glass. Garnish with the maraschino cherry and
orange slice.

 IN MEMORY OF A GREAT BARTENDER,
CHARLIE CHOP • US BARTENDERS' GUILD •
LOS ANGELES, CA

Sauza Breeze Martini

2 oz. Sauza tequila
¼ oz. Chambord
¼ oz. sour mix
Lime for garnish

Shake with ice, and strain into a chilled martini
glass. Serve on the rocks or straight up. Garnish
with the lime.

 GATSBY • BOCA RATON, FL

Savoy Hotel Special Martini

1 ½ oz. dry gin
½ oz. dry vermouth
2 dashes grenadine
Dash Pernod
Lemon twist for garnish

Shake with ice, and strain into a chilled martini
glass. Serve on the rocks or straight up. Garnish
with the twist.

Savoy Martini

1 ¾ oz. dry gin
½ oz. dry vermouth
¼ oz. Dubonnet
Orange peel for garnish

Shake with ice, and strain into a chilled martini glass. Serve on the rocks or straight up. Garnish with the orange peel.

Scarlettini

2 oz. Ketel One vodka
Touch Bonny Doon's raspberry wine

Serve on the rocks.

 GLENN'S RESTAURANT & COOL BAR •
NEWBURYPORT, MA

Schnozzle Martini

¾ oz. dry gin
¾ oz. dry vermouth
½ oz. cocktail sherry
¼ oz. orange curaçao
¼ oz. Pernod

Screamin' Hudson

1 ½ oz. Canadian whisky
½ oz. Drambuie liqueur
½ oz. lemon juice

Shake well with ice, and strain into a martini cocktail glass.

Seduction Martini

2 ½ oz. Smirnoff vodka
⅓ oz. lime juice
Splash Benedictine
Splash brandy
Splash grenadine
Orange wheel for garnish

Shake with ice, and strain into a glass. Garnish with the orange wheel.

Self-Starter Martini

1 ½ oz. dry gin
¾ oz. Lillet
¼ oz. apricot-flavored brandy
2 dashes Pernod

Seventh Heaven Martini

1 ½ oz. gin
½ oz. maraschino cherry juice
½ oz. unsweetened grapefruit juice
Mint sprig
Orange twist for garnish

Shake with ice, and strain into a chilled glass.
Garnish with the mint and orange twist.

Sexual Trance Martini

2 oz. Absolut Citron vodka
¼ oz. Chambord
¼ oz. Midori melon liqueur
¼ oz. orange juice
¼ oz. pineapple juice
¼ oz. sweet and sour
Maraschino cherry for garnish

Shake with ice, and strain into a chilled martini
glass. Serve on the rocks or straight up. Garnish
with the maraschino cherry.

Sexy Back

2 oz. Absolut Citron vodka
¾ oz. Crème Cassis de Dijon
Dash sour mix
Champagne to top

Shake well with ice, and strain into a martini glass. Top with the champagne.

 BRUNO JAMAIS RESTAURANT CLUB • NEW YORK, NY

Sexy Devil

1 oz. Finlandia Arctic Cranberry vodka
    (infused with fresh strawberries)
1 oz. Finlandia vodka
¼ oz. extra dry vermouth
Lemon peel-wrapped Holland pepper for
    garnish

 CENTRO RISTORANTE • CHICAGO, IL

Shaken Not Stirred Martini

1 ½ oz. Tanqueray gin
1 oz. Ketel One vodka
½ oz. Lillet
Lemon twist for garnish

Shake with ice, and strain into a chilled martini glass. Serve on the rocks or straight up.

Sharkbite Martini

2 oz. dry gin
½ oz. Sprite
Squeeze of lemon

Serve on the rocks.

 RED LOBSTER • MEMPHIS, TN

Sharp Susie Martini

1 oz. Finlandia Arctic Cranberry vodka
½ oz. Absolut Citron vodka
½ oz. Absolut Kurant vodka
½ oz. Cointreau
Pearl onion for garnish

Shake well, and pour into an ice-cold cocktail glass. Garnish with the pearl onion.

 KRISU

Sherry Cocktail Martini

2 oz. dry sherry
½ oz. dry vermouth
2 dashes orange bitters

Shake with ice, and strain into a chilled martini glass. Serve on the rocks or straight up.

Shiso & Lime Leaf Martini

3 lime leaves (plus 1 for garnish)
2 shiso leaves (plus 1 for garnish)
Dash sugar syrup
Ketel One vodka

Muddle 3 lime leaves and 2 shiso leaves with a
large dash of sugar syrup. Add a large pour of
Ketel One vodka. Shake well, and strain into martini glass. Garnish with the shiso and lime leaf.

Silk Panties Martini

2 ½ oz. Stolichnaya vodka
½ oz. peach schnapps

Blend until smooth.

Silk Spirit

1 oz. Stolichnaya Vanil vodka
½ oz. Wild Spirit
¼ oz. chocolate liqueur

Serve chilled and straight up.

Silk Rose

1 oz. Tequila Rose
½ oz. banana schnapps
½ oz. butterscotch schnapps
½ oz. milk
¼ oz. half-and-half

Shake with ice, and strain into a small martini glass.

Silken Veil Martini

1 oz. Dubonnet Rouge
1 oz. vodka
Lemon twist for garnish

Chill, strain, and garnish with the lemon twist.

Silver Bikini Martini

2 oz. Gordon's vodka
½ oz. orange juice
Splash Framboise
Raspberry for garnish

Shake with ice, and strain into a martini glass. Garnish with the raspberry.

Silver Bullet Martini

1 ½ oz. Bombay Sapphire gin
Dash Martini & Rossi extra dry vermouth
J&B scotch to float

Shake and strain first two ingredients into a glass. Serve straight up or on the rocks. Float J&B scotch on top.

Silver Sobieski

2 ½ oz. Sobieski vodka
Edible silver flakes for garnish

Serve chilled in a martini glass. Garnish with the edible silver flakes.

Silver Streak Martini

1 ½ oz. dry gin
1 ½ oz. Kummel

Pour over finely crushed ice into a small wine glass.

Simpson Martini

2 oz. vodka
¾ oz. vermouth
Black olive for garnish
Orange peel for garnish

Shake well with ice, and strain into a martini glass.
Garnish with the black olive and sliver of orange
peel speared with a dagger plastic toothpick.

 KAREN PIKE DAVIS • EASTON, PA

Skizzy

1 oz. Finlandia Grapefruit vodka
1 oz. fresh raspberry puree
1 oz. Tanqueray gin
½ oz. fresh lime juice

Shake, and serve in a chilled martini glass.

 STEPHANIE KANTOR • TONY'S BIG EASY BISTRO
• STATE COLLEGE, PA

Sky Martini

2 ½ oz. Skyy vodka
Splash blue curaçao
2 olives for garnish

Shake with ice, and strain into a well-chilled glass. Garnish with the 2 olives.

 THE BOULDER'S INN • ROXBURY, CT

Skyy Blue Buddha

2 oz. Skyy vodka
½ oz. lemon juice
½ oz. lime juice
¼ oz. blue curaçao
¼ oz. grapefruit juice
¼ oz. sake
Splash simple syrup
Fresh orange slice for garnish

 301 SAKE BAR AND RESTAURANT • SAN FRANCISCO, CA

Skyy Citroni

2 oz. Skyy Infusions citrus vodka
Splash Cinzano vermouth
Orange slice to float

Stir with ice. Serve in a chilled martini glass with
an orange slice float.

Skyy High Martini

2 oz. Skyy vodka
½ oz. Chambord
Lemon twist for garnish

 THE WINDSOCK BAR & GRILL • SAN DIEGO, CA

Skyy Irish Black Forest Cake

Sugar to rim
2 oz. Skyy Infusions Cherry vodka
1 oz. chocolate liqueur
½ oz. Carolans Irish cream

Rim a martini glass with sugar. Shake with ice,
and strain into the glass.

Skyy White Chocolate Martini

2 oz. Skyy vodka
½ oz. white crème de cacao

Shake, don't stir. Serve straight up in an over-sized, chilled stem glass.

Skyy-Fi Martini

2 ½ oz. Skyy vodka
½ oz. blue curaçao
½ oz. Midori melon liqueur
Lemon twist for garnish

Chill, and serve straight up garnished with the lemon twist.

 DIANE MOSCATO • 7 CENTRAL PUBLIC HOUSE • MANCHESTER, MA

Sloe Vermouth Martini

1 oz. dry vermouth
1 oz. sloe gin
⅓ oz. fresh lemon juice

Shake with ice, and strain into a chilled glass.

Smashed Pumpkin

1 oz. Godiva original liqueur
½ oz. Cointreau
½ oz. Godet Belgian white chocolate
   liqueur
½ oz. Grey Goose vodka
Chocolate orange slice for garnish

Shake with ice, and strain into a chilled martini glass. Serve on the rocks or straight up. Garnish with the chocolate orange slice.

 JILL RUGGLES AND ERICA HOLM • DRINK •
CHICAGO, IL

Smiler Martini

1 ¼ oz. dry gin
½ oz. dry vermouth
½ oz. sweet vermouth
¼ oz. orange juice
Dash Angostura bitters

Shake with ice, and strain into a chilled martini glass. Serve on the rocks or straight up.

Smirnoff Citrus Valicious

1 ½ oz. pink grapefruit juice
1 ½ oz. Smirnoff citrus vodka
½ oz. pink lemonade
Lemon wedge for garnish

Shake with ice, and strain into a martini glass.
Garnish with the lemon.

Smirnoff Orange Martini

1 ½ oz. Smirnoff citrus vodka
Splash cranberry juice
Splash lime juice
Splash triple sec
Lime twist for garnish

Shake with ice, and strain into a chilled martini
glass. Garnish with the lime twist.

Smirnoff Raspberry Delight

1 ½ oz. lemon-lime soda
1 ½ oz. Smirnoff raspberry vodka
Splash sour mix
Raspberry for garnish

Shake with ice, and strain into a chilled martini
glass. Garnish with the raspberry.

Smirnoff Strawberry Redheaded Martini

Sugar to rim
1 ½ oz. Smirnoff strawberry vodka
Splash cranberry juice
Splash sour mix
Strawberry for garnish

Rim a long drink glass with sugar. Build over ice in the glass. Garnish with the strawberry.

Smoke and Fire Olive Martini

2 oz. Three Olives vodka
½ oz. Laphroaig scotch
Garlic-jalapeño red pepper olive for garnish

Shake with ice, and strain into a chilled martini glass. Garnish with the garlic-jalapeño red pepper olive.

 BOB BRUNNER • PARAGON RESTAURANT & BAR
• PORTLAND, OR

Smokey Martini

2 oz. Tanqueray gin
¼ oz. scotch
Lemon twist for garnish

Shake with ice, and strain into a chilled martini glass. Serve straight up or on the rocks.

Smokey Martini II

¼ oz. high-quality whiskey
2 ½ oz. vodka

Coat a martini glass with a good whiskey, and discard excess. Make a normal vodka martini (shaken not stirred); add to the glass.

 MARK WIJMAN • ALMERE • THE NETHERLANDS

Smokey Mountain Martini

1 ½ oz. Finlandia vodka
¼ oz. Knob Creek bourbon

Shake with ice, and strain into a martini glass.

 BRETT EGAN, DIRECTOR • NATIONAL BARTENDERS
SCHOOL • LAKEWOOD, CA

Smooth Martini

2 oz. Ketel One vodka

Fill shaker with half ice cubes and half shaved ice. Shake, and strain into a chilled martini glass.

S'more Martini

Cinnamon to rim
2 oz. Finlandia vodka
½ oz. chocolate liqueur
⅛ oz. Martini & Rossi Rosso sweet vermouth

Shake with ice, and strain into a chilled martini glass. Rim a glass with cinnamon, and serve.

Snowball Martini

1 ½ oz. gin
½ oz. cream
½ oz. Pernod or other anise-flavored
   liqueur

Shake with ice, and strain into a chilled glass.

Snowcone Martini

1 oz. Bacardi Seven Tiki rum
1 oz. banana liqueur
½ oz. blue curaçao
Mist Martini & Rossi extra dry vermouth

Garnish with a large ball of ice in the middle of
the cocktail.

 MICHAEL JORDAN'S • CHICAGO, IL

Snyder Martini

1 ¾ oz. dry gin
½ oz. dry vermouth
¼ oz. orange curaçao
Orange peel for garnish

Shake with ice, and strain into a chilled martini
glass. Serve on the rocks or straight up.

So Be It

2 ½ oz. Sobieski vodka
½ oz. amaretto
½ oz. Baileys Irish cream

Shake with ice, and strain. Serve straight up in a
martini glass.

The So Damn Delicious Birthdaytini

2 oz. Grande Absente
½ oz. triple sec
1 tsp. sugar
Lime slice or twist for garnish

Shake with ice until cold, and strain into a martini glass. Garnish by floating a lime slice or drip in a lime twist.

So-Co-Martini

2 oz. Southern Comfort
¼ oz. dry vermouth
¼ oz. sweet vermouth
Maraschino cherry for garnish

Solar Flare Martini

1 ½ oz. Tanqueray gin
¼ oz. dry vermouth
5 drops crème de noyeaux
Maraschino cherry stem for garnish

Shake the first two ingredients, and strain into a glass. Add crème de noyeaux. Garnish with the maraschino cherry stem.

 DOUG BRAVO • TEXAS STATION HOTEL & CASINO • LAS VEGAS, NV

Some Like It Hot Martini

2 oz. Absolut Peppar vodka
Red chili pepper for garnish

Shake with ice, and strain into a chilled martini glass. Serve on the rocks or straight up. Garnish with the chili pepper.

Sonic Gold Martini

1 ½ oz. Campari
1 ½ oz. Stolichnaya Gold vodka
Splash cranberry juice
Splash tonic
Soda water to fill
Orange slice for garnish

Pour first four ingredients over ice in a tall glass.
Fill with soda water. Stir, and garnish with the
orange slice.

 C3 RESTAURANT & LOUNGE • NEW YORK, NY

Sour Apple Martini

2 oz. Grey Goose vodka
½ oz. DeKuyper Sour Apple Pucker
  schnapps
Slice of Granny Smith apple for garnish

Shake with ice, and strain into a chilled martini
glass. Serve on the rocks or straight up. Garnish
with the apple slice.

 MICHAEL WALLER • MARTUNI'S •
SAN FRANCISCO, CA

Sour Patch Martini

2 oz. Stolichnaya Ohranj vodka
2 oz. Stolichnaya Razberi vodka
2 oz. Stolichnaya Strasberi vodka
2 oz. Stolichnaya vodka
Splash grenadine
Splash orange juice
Splash pineapple juice
Splash sour mix

Shake with ice, and strain into a chilled martini
glass. Serve on the rocks or straight up.

 GATSBY • BOCA RATON, FL

South Beach

2 oz. Bacardi rum
½ oz. Malibu
½ oz. pineapple juice
¼ oz. blue curaçao

Shake with ice, and strain into a chilled martini
glass. Serve on the rocks or straight up.

 GATSBY • BOCA RATON, FL

Southern Gin Cocktail Martini

2 ¼ oz. dry gin
¼ oz. orange curaçao
2 dashes orange bitters

Shake with ice, and strain into a chilled martini glass. Serve on the rocks or straight up.

Soviet Martini

2 oz. Smirnoff vodka
½ oz. Manzanilla sherry
Splash dry vermouth
Lemon twist for garnish

Chill, and strain into a glass. Garnish with the lemon twist.

Soviet Slush

2 parts Stolichnaya Ohranj vodka
1 part Black Haus Blackberry schnapps
1 part gin
1 part Rumple Minze
2 scoops rainbow sherbet
Kiwi fruit for garnish
Mint leaf for garnish

Mix in a blender, and serve in a hurricane glass. Garnish with the piece of kiwi fruit and the mint leaf.

 ERIC MORRIS • MULLIGAN'S, SALISBURY • MD

Spanish Martini

1 ½ oz. gin
½ oz. dry sack sherry
Lemon twist for garnish

Shake with ice, and strain into a chilled martini glass. Serve on the rocks or straight up. Garnish with the lemon twist.

Sparkling Raspberry Martini

2 oz. Stolichnaya Razberi vodka
½ oz. Massenez Crème de Framboise
½ oz. Domaine Chandon Brut Rosé

Shake the first two ingredients with ice, and strain into a chilled martini glass. Top with Domaine Chandon Brut Rosé.

 BUBBLE LOUNGE • NEW YORK, NY

Sphinx Martini

2 oz. Beefeater gin
¾ oz. Martini & Rossi extra dry vermouth
¼ oz. Martini & Rossi Rosso sweet vermouth
Lemon wedge for garnish

Spiaggi

2 oz. Stolichnaya Vanil vodka
¼ oz. Tuaca Italian liqueur

Shake with ice, and strain into a chilled martini glass. Serve on the rocks or straight up.

Spiced Oyster Martini

Fresh Kumamoto oyster
1 small jalapeño pepper
Tabasco sauce
Lemon juice
2 oz. frozen Belvedere vodka

Cover the oyster with the jalapeño, Tabasco sauce, lemon juice, and vodka.

Spicy Hard Shell Favorite

1 ½ oz. Stolichnaya vodka
3 dashes Texas Pete hot sauce

Shake with ice, and strain into a chilled martini glass. Serve on the rocks or straight up.

JEFF MCCARTHY • THE HARD SHELL • RICHMOND, VA

Spiked Lilly

2 oz. Belvedere vodka
½ oz. Cranberry juice
½ oz. Orange juice
½ oz. Sprite

Shake the first three ingredients with ice, and strain into a chilled martini glass. Top with Sprite.

 LILY'S RESTAURANT • NEW YORK, NY

St. Tropez Martini

1 ½ oz. Smirnoff vodka
Splash orange juice
Splash peach schnapps
Dash grenadine
Peach wedge

Chill, and strain into a glass. Garnish with the peach wedge.

Stake Martini

2 oz. Sobieski vodka
¼ oz. gin
¼ oz. sake
Cucumber slice for garnish

Shake with ice, and strain into the chilled martini glass. Garnish with the cucumber.

Stang Bill Martini

Splash The Famous Grouse whisky
1 ½ oz. Tanqueray gin
Olives for garnish

Wash a martini glass with The Famous Grouse.
Shake gin with ice. Roll the shaker with gin back
and forth, mixing gin into the ice. Top the shaker
with ice, and strain gin into a glass, using ice as
a strainer. Garnish with olives.

 BILL STANG, BARTENDER • THE BLACKDUCK
FREEHOUSE • SASKATCHEWAN, BC

Star Cocktail Martini

1 ½ oz. apple brandy
1 ½ oz. sweet vermouth
2 dashes Angostura bitters
Lemon twist for garnish

Stir with ice, and strain into a chilled glass.
Garnish with the lemon twist.

Star Tini

Splash Martini & Rossi extra dry vermouth
2 ½ oz. Stolichnaya vodka
½ oz. Campari
Orange twist for garnish

Rinse a glass with the vermouth. Add the remaining ingredients, and garnish with the orange twist.

 HARRY DENTON'S STARLIGHT ROOM • SAN FRANCISCO, CA

Starburst Martini

2 oz. Grey Goose vodka
1 oz. strawberry liqueur
½ oz. pineapple juice
½ oz. sour mix
Pinch sugar
Strawberry for garnish

Mix all ingredients, and shake vigorously. Garnish with the strawberry.

 "SMILEY" • BASH NIGHTCLUB • MIAMI, FL

Starlight Martini

1 ¾ oz. Beefeater gin
¾ oz. orange curaçao
Dash Angostura bitters

Shake with ice, and strain into a chilled martini glass. Serve on the rocks or straight up.

Starry Night

2 oz. Vincent Van Gogh vodka
½ oz. blue curaçao
Splash sweet and sour mix
Lemon twist for garnish

Combine ingredients, and pour into a martini glass. Garnish with the lemon twist.

 ANDY PORTER • VAN GOGH'S RESTAURANT & BAR • ATLANTA, GA

Stefano Martini

1 ½ oz. Smirnoff vodka
Dash grenadine
Lemonade to float

Chill with ice, and strain into a martini glass. Float the lemonade.

Stick 'Em Up

2 oz. Sobieski vodka
¼ oz. DeKuyper Cactus Juice Burst

Shake with ice, and strain into a chilled martini glass. Serve on the rocks or straight up.

Still Life Martini

2 oz. Smirnoff vodka
¼ oz. Baileys Irish cream
¼ oz. coffee liqueur
Maraschino cherry for garnish
Orange wheel for garnish

Shake with ice, and strain into a glass. Garnish with the maraschino cherry and orange wheel.

Stoli Bellini Martini

2 oz. Stolichnaya Peachik vodka
¼ oz. peach schnapps
Champagne

Stir. Serve in a chilled martini glass.

Stoli Bikini Martini

2 ½ oz. Stolichnaya Ohranj vodka
Generous splash Framboise
Raspberry for garnish

Shake or stir vigorously with ice, and serve in a chilled martini glass. Garnish with the raspberry.

Stoli Grand Martini

2 oz. dry vermouth
1 ½ oz. Stolichnaya Ohranj vodka
¼ oz. Grand Marnier

Pour vermouth into a tumbler with crushed ice, and drain off. Swirl remaining ingredients in tumbler for 2–3 minutes until silky.

 JAY TARANTINO • TAVERNE ON THE LAKE •
LAWRENCEBURG, IN

Stoli Hummer

2 oz. orange juice
1 oz. amaretto
1 oz. Bacardi rum
1 oz. Stolichnaya Vanil vodka
½ oz. grenadine

Shake with ice, and strain into a tall glass filled with ice.

 ANDREW THOMPSON • ROCK & KATH'S SAWMILL

Stoli Power Martini

3 oz. orange juice
1 ½ oz. Stolichnaya Ohranj vodka
1 oz. raspberry syrup
½ oz. lemon juice
Orange peel for garnish

Shake with ice, and strain into a chilled glass. Garnish with the orange peel.

Stolichnaya Paradise Martini

2 parts Stolichnaya Ohranj vodka
1 part orange juice
Orange slice for garnish

Shake with ice, and strain into a martini glass. Garnish with the orange slice.

Straight Law Martini

1 ¾ oz. dry sherry
¾ oz. dry gin
Champagne to top
Lemon twist for garnish

Strawberry Blintz Martini

Sugar to rim
2 oz. Stolichnaya Strasberi vodka
Splash cranberry juice
White chocolate-dipped strawberry for
    garnish

Rim a martini glass with sugar. Shake with
ice, and strain into the glass. Garnish with the
strawberry.

Strawberry Blonde Martini

2 oz. Beefeater gin
1 oz. Chambraise strawberry aperitif
Lemon twist for garnish

Strawberry Chocolate Martini

1 ½ oz. strawberry liqueur
1 ½ oz. white crème de cacao
Strawberry for garnish

Shake with ice, and strain into a chilled martini glass. Serve on the rocks or straight up. Garnish with the strawberry.

 JOSEPH VUCKOVIC • RUSSO'S ON THE BAY • HOWARD BEACH, NY

Strawberry Martini

1 ½ oz. dry gin
1 oz. Fragoli
Fresh strawberry for garnish

Blend and stir.

Strawberry Shortcake Martini

Crushed graham cracker to rim glass
1 ½ oz. Fragoli
1 oz. vanilla vodka
½ oz. white crème de cacao

Rim a glass with crushed graham cracker crumbs. Shake with ice, and strain into the glass.

String of Pearls

2 ½ oz. Leyden gin
4 cocktail onions for garnish

 BILL CHIUSANO • BLOOMFIELD, NJ

Submarine Martini

1 ½ oz. Beefeater dry gin
½ oz. Dubonnet
½ oz. Martini & Rossi extra dry vermouth
Dash Boker's bitters

Shake with ice, and strain into a chilled martini
glass. Serve on the rocks or straight up.

Sugar Magnolia Dark Martini

1 ¼ oz. vodka
¾ oz. dark crème de cacao
Hershey's Kiss for garnish

Shake with ice, and strain into a chilled martini
glass. Serve on the rocks or straight up. Garnish
with the Hershey's Kiss.

Summer Scotch Martini

2 oz. Bunnahabhain scotch
2 oz. grapefruit
½ oz. dry vermouth
Lemon twist for garnish

Shake all ingredients with ice and strain into a chilled martini glass. Garnish with the lemon twist.

Summertime Martini

1 ¼ oz. Gordon's grapefruit gin
1 ¼ oz. Stolichnaya Ohranj vodka
½ oz. Chambord
Flag for garnish

Shake with ice, and strain into a glass. Serve straight up or on the rocks. Garnish with the flag.

 CHARLIE'S ON THE LAKE • OMAHA, NE

Sunburst Martini

2 ½ oz. 4 Orange vodka
⅛ oz. dry vermouth
Orange slice for garnish

Sundowner Martini

2 ½ oz. orange juice
2 oz. Stolichnaya Razberi vodka
¼ oz. cranberry juice
1 or 2 splashes grenadine

Shake orange juice and vodka with ice, and strain into a glass. Add the cranberry juice and grenadine.

Sunflower

2 oz. Vincent Van Gogh vodka
½ oz. Grand Marnier
Splash blood orange juice
Blood orange wedge for garnish
Edible flowers for garnish

Combine the first three ingredients, and shake with ice. Garnish with the blood orange wedge and edible flowers.

 ANDY PORTER • VAN GOGH'S RESTAURANT & BAR
• ATLANTA, GA

Sunrise Martini

2 oz. Smirnoff vodka
1 oz. Cuervo 1800 tequila
Splash Grand Marnier
Splash grenadine
Orange slice for garnish

Shake with ice, and strain into a chilled martini
glass. Serve on the rocks or straight up. Garnish
with the orange slice.

Sunset

2 oz. Stolichnaya Ohranj vodka
3 dashes Angostura bitters
Orange slice for garnish

Shake with ice, and strain into a chilled martini
glass. Serve on the rocks or straight up. Garnish
with the orange slice.

Super Juice Martini

2 ½ oz. Stolichnaya Ohranj vodka
½ oz. cranberry juice
½ oz. orange juice

Shake with ice, and strain into a chilled martini
glass. Serve on the rocks or straight up.

Super Model

2 oz. Bacardi Limón rum
½ oz. blue curaçao
½ oz. melon liqueur
Splash Martini & Rossi extra dry vermouth

Shake ingredients with ice, and strain into a chilled glass.

Supper Martini

2 oz. Boodles British Gin
Dash Drambuie
Dash Martini & Rossi Rosso sweet vermouth
Maraschino cherry for garnish

Shake with ice, and strain into a chilled martini glass. Garnish with the maraschino cherry.

 MUMBO JUMBO • ATLANTA, GA

Supreme Chocolate Martini

Unsweetened cocoa powder to rim
Hershey's Kiss candy
2 oz. vodka
1 ½ oz. Marie Brizard white crème de cacao

Rim a martini glass with cocoa powder, and place the Kiss pointed top up in the bottom of the glass. Stir ingredients with ice until well chilled, and strain into the glass.

 MARIE BRIZARD • FLORIDA

Surfer Martini

1 ½ oz. Smirnoff vodka
½ oz. Malibu coconut rum
Splash banana liqueur
Pineapple wedge for garnish

Chill with ice, and strain into a glass. Garnish with the pineapple wedge.

Sushi Martini

2 ½ oz. Tanqueray gin
¼ oz. Martini & Rossi extra dry vermouth
Pickled ginger for garnish
Tobiko-stuffed olive for garnish

Serve straight up with the pickled ginger and Tobiko-stuffed olive.

Sweet Arlene

¼ oz. apple cider
¼ oz. gin
¼ oz. limoncello
¼ oz. Martini & Rossi Rosso sweet vermouth
Dash bitters
Apple slice for garnish

Shake with ice, and strain into a chilled martini glass. Serve on the rocks or straight up. Garnish with the apple slice.

 STEVE VISAKAY • VINTAGE COCKTAIL SHAKERS

Sweet Dutchman

2 parts sweet vermouth
1 part Leyden gin
Orange peel for garnish

Shake with ice, and strain into a chilled martini
glass. Serve on the rocks or straight up. Garnish
with the orange peel.

 BILL CHIUSANO • UPPER MONTCLAIR, NJ

Sweet Martini

1 ½ oz. Absolut Citron vodka
¼ oz. extra dry vermouth
Splash Chambord
Lemon twist for garnish

Shake well with ice, and strain into a martini
glass. Garnish with the lemon twist.

 JANE LOMSHEK, BARTENDER • HOLIDOME •
LAWRENCE, KS

Swiss Kiss Martini

2 oz. Grey Goose vodka
1 oz. crème de cacao
½ oz. butterscotch schnapps
½ oz. Frangelico
Godet white chocolate liqueur to drizzle
Godiva chocolate for garnish

Shake the first four ingredients with ice, and strain into a chilled martini glass. Lace with white chocolate liqueur, and sprinkle with Godiva chocolate.

 IRAKLIS PAPACHRISTOS OF MERCURY BAR • BOSTON, MA

Take Off Martini

2 ½ oz. Tanqueray gin
¼ oz. Cointreau
Orange peel for garnish

Shake with ice, and strain into a chilled martini glass. Serve on the rocks or straight up. Garnish with the orange peel.

Tall, Dark, & Handsome

½ oz. crème de cacao
½ oz. DeKuyper But   Butershots schnapps
½ oz. Thrilla Vanilla liqueur
½ oz. vodka
Chocolate syrup to decorate glass

Serve in a glass lightly drizzled with chocolate syrup.

 MINDY MOLLER • EMAILED TO OUR BLOG, WWW. BARTENDERMAGAZINE.WORDPRESS.COM

Tangerine Delight

2 ½ oz. Stolichnaya Ohranj vodka
¼ oz. dark crème de cacao
Orange twist for garnish

Chill, and serve straight up. Garnish with the orange twist.

Tango Cocktail Martini

1 oz. gin
½ oz. fresh orange juice
½ oz. Martini & Rossi Rosso sweet vermouth
½ oz. Martini & Rossi vermouth
½ tsp. triple sec

Shake with ice, and strain into a chilled glass.

Tanqueray Extra Dry Martini

2 ½ oz. Tanqueray gin
¼ oz. dry vermouth
Olive for garnish

Serve straight up in a chilled martini glass.
Garnish with the olive.

Tanqueray No. Ten Martini

2 ¼ oz. Tanqueray No. Ten
1 ¾ oz. lime juice
Squeeze lime wedge

Shake with ice, and strain into a chilled martini
glass. Serve on the rocks or straight up.

Tanqueray No. Ten Rickey

5 oz. fresh lime juice
1 ½ oz. Tanqueray No. Ten
1 oz. sour mix
Splash soda
Lime slice for garnish

Shake the first three ingredients with ice, and
strain into a frosted martini glass. Top with soda.
Garnish with the lime slice.

 J. NESS • NEW YORK, NY

411

Tanqueray "Perfect Ten" Martini

2 oz. Tanqueray No. Ten
1 oz. Grand Marnier
½ oz. sour mix

Shake with ice, and strain into a chilled martini glass. Serve on the rocks or straight up.

Tanqy Breezy Martini

3 oz. Tanqueray gin
1 oz. grapefruit juice
1 oz. pineapple juice
Dash dry vermouth
Lemon twist or olive for garnish

Shake with ice, and strain into a chilled martini glass. Serve on the rocks or straight up. Garnish with the lemon twist or olive.

 HYMAN GOLDFELD • PHILADELPHIA, PA

Tantra Kiss

3 oz. Grey Goose vodka
1 oz. peach schnapps
Splash cranberry juice
Splash pineapple juice
Edible pansy for garnish

Shake with ice, and strain into a glass. Serve straight up. Garnish with the edible pansy.

 BRUCE CRAIG • TANTRA, INC. • MIAMI, FL

Tapika's Martini

2 ½ oz. Chinaco Blanco tequila
½ oz. Cointreau
½ oz. Martini & Rossi extra dry vermouth
Lime wedge for garnish

Shake with ice, and strain into a chilled martini glass. Serve on the rocks or straight up. Garnish with the lime wedge.

 REEBOK SPORTS CLUB • NEW YORK, NY

Taropolitan

3 oz. cranberry juice
2 oz. Tarantula Reposado tequila
Splash lime juice

Shake with ice, and strain into a chilled martini
glass.

Tartini

1 ½ oz. Stolichnaya Razberi vodka
Dash Chambord
Dash Rose's Lime Juice
Splash cranberry juice
Lime wedge for garnish

Tatou's Tatouni

2 ½ oz. Ketel One vodka
¼ oz. Martini & Rossi extra dry vermouth
⅛ oz. cucumber juice
Cucumber slices to garnish

Shake with ice, and strain into a chilled martini
glass. Serve on the rocks or straight up. Garnish
with the cucumber.

Teeny Weeny Chocolate Martini

2 oz. Ketel One vodka
¼ oz. white crème de cacao
Chocolate truffle for garnish

Shake with ice, and strain into a chilled martini glass. Serve on the rocks or straight up. Garnish with the truffle.

Temple-Tini

2 oz. Absolut Kurant vodka
¼ oz. Chambord
Maraschino cherry for garnish

Shake with ice, and strain into a chilled martini glass. Serve on the rocks or straight up. Garnish with the maraschino cherry.

Tequila Gimlet Martini

2 oz. Patrón tequila
1 oz. lime juice
Lime wedge for garnish

Chill, and strain into a glass. Garnish with the lime wedge.

Tequila Martini

2 oz. Patrón tequila
¼ oz. Cointreau

Shake with ice, and strain into a chilled martini glass. Serve on the rocks or straight up.

Tequina Martini

2 oz. Patrón tequila
½ oz. dry vermouth
Lemon twist for garnish

Stir with ice until chilled, and strain into a chilled cocktail glass. Garnish with the lemon twist.

Thai Martini

2 oz. Smirnoff vodka
3 stalks lemongrass, lightly crushed
1 cilantro stem for garnish

Infuse vodka with lemongrass. Chill, and strain into a glass. Garnish with the fresh cilantro.

That's Italian Martini

2 ½ oz. Ketel One vodka
½ oz. Campari
Orange and lemon slices for garnish

Shake with ice, and strain into a chilled martini glass. Serve on the rocks or straight up. Garnish with the orange and lemon slices.

Thigh Opener

2 oz. vodka
¼ oz. lime juice
¼ oz. triple sec

Shake with ice, and strain into a glass. Serve on the rocks.

Third Degree Martini

Bottle Smirnoff vodka
Jalapeño pepper seeds
Pickled yellow pepper for garnish

Infuse vodka with jalapeño pepper seeds intact. Thoroughly chill vodka in the freezer. Strain into a chilled martini glass, and garnish with the pickled yellow pepper.

Three Continents Martini

1 ¼ oz. Skyy vodka
¼ oz. Grand Marnier
2 drops blue curaçao
Orange twist for garnish

Shake with ice, and strain into a chilled martini glass. Garnish with the orange twist.

 CLIFF INN • EL PASO, TX

Thrilla in Vanilla

2 oz. Sobieski Vanilla vodka
½ oz. peach schnapps

Shake with ice, and strain into a martini glass. Serve straight up.

 L. SACCONE • BASKING RIDGE, NJ

Thrust Martini

Hennessy VS cognac
Dash lemon juice
Lemon peel for garnish

Shake with ice, and strain into a chilled martini
glass. Serve on the rocks or straight up. Garnish
with the lemon peel.

 THE WINDSOCK BAR & GRILL • SAN DIEGO, CA

Tiger-Tini

2 ½ oz. Stolichnaya Ohranj vodka
½ oz. Grand Marnier
Splash orange juice

Shake with ice, and strain into a chilled martini
glass. Serve on the rocks or straight up.

 THE DINER ON SYCAMORE • CINCINNATI, OH

Tijuanatini

2 oz. Ketel One vodka
¼ oz. Kahlúa
Coffee beans for garnish

Shake with ice, and strain into a chilled martini glass. Serve on the rocks or straight up. Garnish with the coffee beans.

 CECILIA'S • BRECKENRIDGE, CO

Tio Pepe Martini

2 oz. dry gin
½ oz. Tio Pepe sherry
Lemon twist for garnish

Shake with ice, and strain into a chilled martini glass. Serve on the rocks or straight up. Garnish with the lemon twist.

Toasted Almond Martini

2 ½ oz. Stolichnaya Vanil vodka
½ oz. Kahlúa
Splash amaretto
Almond or hazelnut for garnish

Shake with ice, and strain into a chilled martini glass. Serve on the rocks or straight up. Garnish with the almond or hazelnut.

Tonight or Never Martini

1 oz. dry gin
1 oz. dry vermouth
½ oz. cognac

Shake with ice, and strain into a chilled martini glass. Serve on the rocks or straight up.

Topaz Martini

1 ¾ oz. Bacardi Limón rum
¼ oz. Martini & Rossi extra dry vermouth
Splash blue curaçao

Combine in a cocktail glass.

Topaz Martini II

2 oz. Gordon's vodka
½ oz. dark crème de cacao
½ oz. Frangelico
3 whole roasted coffee beans to float

Shake with ice, and strain into a chilled martini glass. Serve on the rocks or straight up. Float 3 whole roasted coffee beans.

Tres Martini

Splash Cointreau
1 ½ oz. Tres Generaciones Añejo tequila
Orange zest for garnish

Rinse a chilled martini glass with a splash of Cointreau, and discard. Place Tres Generaciones in a shaker. Fill with ice, shake, and strain into the prepared glass. Garnish with the orange zest.

Trilby Martini

1 ¼ oz. dry gin
1 oz. sweet vermouth
2 dashes orange bitters
¼ oz. crème de Yvette or Chambord

Stir the first three ingredients. Float crème de Yvette or Chambord on top.

Trinity Martini aka Trio Plaza Martini

1 oz. Bombay Sapphire gin
½ oz. extra dry vermouth
½ oz. Martini & Rossi Rosso sweet vermouth
Lemon twist or olives for garnish

Stir with ice, and strain into a cocktail glass. Serve straight up or on the rocks. Garnish with the lemon twist or olives.

Triple G Martini

2 oz. Grey Goose vodka
1 oz. Godet Belgian white chocolate liqueur or white chocolate liqueur
Dash Hershey's syrup (plus more for garnish)

Shake gently. Garnish with Hershey's syrup.

 ERICA FRENE • THE RACK • BOSTON, MA

Tropical Martini

1 ½ oz. Smirnoff vodka
Splash Malibu rum
Splash pineapple juice
Pineapple wedge for garnish

Chill, and strain into a glass. Garnish with the pineapple.

Tropical Martini II

2 oz. Malibu or Captain Morgan's Parrot
   Bay coconut rum
½ oz. pineapple juice
Splash Rose's Lime Juice
Dash salt
Fruit of your choice for garnish

Shake, add ice, shake again, and strain into a chilled martini glass. Garnish with whatever fruit is available.

 AMANDA • EMAILED TO OUR BLOG, WWW.
BARTENDERMAGAZINE.WORDPRESS.COM

Tropical Martini III

1 ½ oz. Stolichnaya Ohranj vodka
1 ½ oz. Stolichnaya Vanil vodka
½ oz. pineapple juice

Shake with ice, and strain into a chilled martini glass. Serve on the rocks or straight up.

Tropical Spellbinder

2 oz. Absolut Citron vodka
½ oz. blue curaçao
½ oz. Midori melon liqueur

Shake with ice, and strain into a chilled martini glass. Serve on the rocks or straight up.

Tropitini Martini

2 oz. pineapple juice
1 oz. Bacardi Limón rum
1 oz. Finlandia vodka
¼ oz. blue curaçao
⅛ oz. Martini & Rossi extra dry vermouth
Pineapple wedge for garnish

Shake with ice, and strain into a glass. Garnish with the pineapple.

Truffle

2 oz. Absolut Kurant vodka
¼ oz. crème de cacao

Shake with ice, and strain into a chilled martini glass. Serve on the rocks or straight up.

 PORTLAND'S BEST • PORTLAND, OR

Truffle Martini

2 ½ oz. Sobieski
Splash of Urbani Tartufi white truffle oil
 (www.urbani.com)

Shake or stir, and serve in a chilled martini glass.

Tulip Cocktail

¾ oz. apple brandy
¾ oz. sweet vermouth
⅓ oz. apricot brandy
1 ½ tsp. fresh lemon juice

Shake ingredients with cracked ice, and strain into a chilled glass.

The Tully 12

¼ oz. dry sherry
1 ½ oz. Tullamore Dew 12-Year-Old
½ oz. dry vermouth
½ oz. sweet vermouth
Dash Angostura bitters

Wash a martini glass with sherry, and discard. Stir with ice, and strain into the glass.

Turantini

1 ½ oz. Tarantula tequila
¼ oz. Cointreau
Splash Rose's Lime Juice
Lime twist for garnish

Shake with ice, and strain into a chilled martini glass. Serve on the rocks or straight up. Garnish with the lime twist.

 PEGASUS • SAN ANTONIO, TX

Tuscan Tini

3 oz. Grey Goose Le Citron vodka
1 oz. limoncello
¾ oz. fresh mint-infused simple syrup
Splash grenadine
Lemon twist for garnish
Fresh mint for garnish

Shake the first three ingredients vigorously over ice. Pour grenadine into the bottom of a chilled martini glass. Pour other ingredients on top of the grenadine. Garnish with the lemon twist and fresh mint.

 TUSCANY GRILL • MIDDLETOWN, CT

Tuxedo Martini

1 ¼ oz. Beefeater gin
1 ¼ oz. Martini & Rossi extra dry vermouth
¼ oz. maraschino cherry juice
¼ tsp. Pernod
2 dashes orange bitters
Lemon twist for garnish

Shake with ice, and strain into a chilled martini glass. Serve on the rocks or straight up. Garnish with the lemon twist.

Twisted Breeze Martini

1 ½ oz. Smirnoff citrus vodka
Dash cranberry juice
Dash grapefruit juice
Fresh cranberries for garnish

Chill, strain, and garnish with the fresh cranberries.

Twisted Citrus Martini

2 oz. Smirnoff citrus vodka, frozen
Lemon wedges for garnish
Lime wedges for garnish

Chill with ice, and strain into a glass. Garnish with large wedges of lemon and lime squeezed into the vodka.

Twisted Hound Martini

1 ½ oz. Smirnoff vodka
Splash freshly squeezed pink grapefruit
   juice

Stir with ice, and strain into a well-chilled martini glass.

Twisted Plaza Martini

1 ½ oz. Smirnoff citrus vodka
Dash melon liqueur
Splash orange juice
Splash pineapple juice
Pineapple wedge for garnish

Chill with ice, and strain into a glass. Garnish with the fresh pineapple wedge.

Twisted-Tini

2 ½ oz. Smirnoff citrus vodka
⅛ oz. dry vermouth

Shake, and do not stir. Strain into a glass, and serve.

Twisting Kurant

2 oz. Absolut Kurant vodka
Big splash sweet vermouth
Sugar-coated lemon twist for garnish

Strain into a chilled martini glass. Garnish with the lemon twist.

 OLIVE GARDEN • LINCOLN, NE

Two Lips Martini

2 ½ oz. Leyden gin
¼ oz. Chambord

Shake with ice, and strain into a chilled martini glass. Serve on the rocks or straight up.

Tyne's Martini

3 shots vodka
Dash Captain Morgan's rum
Lemon twist for garnish

Shake vodka gently with ice. Add rum. Strain into a chilled martini glass. Serve on the rocks or straight up.

 TYNE CAOUETTE • PORTAGE, MI

The Ultimate Blue Cosmopolitan

2 oz. cranberry juice
1 ½ oz. Ultimat vodka
1 oz. blue curaçao
½ oz. Patrón Citrónge Extra Fine Orange
  liqueur
Orange slice for garnish

Shake with ice, and strain into a chilled martini glass. Serve on the rocks or straight up. Garnish with the orange slice.

Ultimate Chill

2 ½ oz. Bombay Sapphire gin or
    Stolichnaya Gold vodka
¼ oz. Cinzano dry vermouth
2 large vermouth-marinated Italian olives
    for garnish

 MARCUS NATES & STEVE BURNEY • OLIVER'S IN
MAYFLOWER PARK HOTEL • SEATTLE, WA

The Ultimate "Envelope Please"

3 oz. fresh apple juice
2 oz. fresh lime juice
1 ½ oz. Ultimat Vodka
½ oz. Patrón Citrónge Extra Fine Orange
    liqueur
Dash cranberry juice
Apple slice for garnish

Shake with ice, and strain into a chilled martini
glass. Serve on the rocks or straight up. Garnish
with the apple slice.

Ultimate Martini

1 oz. Stolichnaya vodka
½ oz. Campari
¼ oz. sweet vermouth

Shake with ice, and strain into a chilled martini glass. Serve on the rocks or straight up.

Ultimate Martini II

2 ½ oz. Boodles British dry gin
⅛ oz. dry vermouth
Queen olives stuffed with Stilton cheese
    for garnish

Shake with ice, and strain into a chilled martini glass. Serve on the rocks or straight up.

 POLO LOUNGE • WINDSOR COURT HOTEL •
NEW ORLEANS, LA

Under the Volcano Martini

2 ½ oz. The Encantado Martini—100 per-
    cent Mescal
½ oz. Martini & Rossi vermouth
Jalapeño-stuffed olive for garnish

Union League Martini

1 ¾ oz. Old Tom gin
¾ oz. port wine
Dash orange bitters

Shake with ice, and strain into a chilled martini glass. Serve on the rocks or straight up.

The Uniquesituation

4 oz. pineapple juice
1 oz. Bacardi Limón rum
1 oz. Midori melon liqueur
Maraschino cherry for garnish

Shake with ice, and strain into a martini glass. Garnish with the cherry.

 TERRY BEISEL • THE BUBBLE LOUNGE • MOBILE, AL

Up Up & Away

Beefeater gin
Splash grapefruit juice
Lemon twist for garnish

Shake with ice, and strain into a chilled martini glass. Serve on the rocks or straight up. Garnish with the lemon twist.

 THE WINDSOCK BAR & GRILL • SAN DIEGO, CA

Uptown Alizé

2 oz. Alizé Red Passion liqueur
2 oz. Hennessy cognac

Strain into a glass, and serve over ice.

 SIDNEY MASTERS • THE SHARK BAR • NEW YORK, NY

USA Martini

2 ½ oz. Teton Glacier Potato vodka—made
    in the USA
⅛ oz. vermouth

USA, Prince of Martini

¾ oz. vodka
½ oz. Wild Spirit
Dash vermouth
Orange wheel for garnish

Shake with ice, and strain into a chilled martini
glass. Serve on the rocks or straight up. Garnish
with the orange wheel.

 STEVE PRINCE • EMAILED TO OUR BLOG, WWW.
BARTENDERMAGAZINE.WORDPRESS.COM

Usabay Martini

1 ¾ oz. vodka
½ oz. Captain Morgan's Parrot Bay
   Coconut rum
Coconut twist for garnish

 CHRIS HAMMOND • EMAILED TO OUR BLOG,
WWW.BARTENDERMAGAZINE.WORDPRESS.COM

Valerie

2 oz. Tanqueray gin
⅛ oz. olive juice
2 olives for garnish

Shake with ice, and strain into a chilled martini
glass. Serve on the rocks or straight up. Top with
the olives.

 WENDY MICHAELS • BRANDING IRON • YAMHILL, OR

Vampire Martini

2 oz. Stolichnaya vodka
½ oz. Chambord
Touch cranberry juice

Shake with ice, and strain into a chilled martini
glass. Serve on the rocks or straight up.

Van Martini

1 ¾ oz. Bombay Sapphire gin
½ oz. Martini & Rossi extra dry vermouth
¼ oz. Grand Marnier

Shake with ice, and strain into a chilled martini glass. Serve on the rocks or straight up.

Vanilla Beani

1 oz. Stolichnaya Vanil vodka
Splash Tuaca
Vanilla bean for garnish

Shake with ice, and strain into a chilled martini glass. Serve on the rocks or straight up. Garnish with the vanilla bean.

 PEGGY HOWELL • COTATI YACHT CLUB & SALOON • COTATI, CA

Vanilla Rain

1 part Dr. Vanillacuddy schnapps, chilled
1 part Rain vodka, chilled

Shake with ice, and strain into a martini glass.

Veggie Martini

2 ½ oz. Tanqueray gin
Baby carrots for garnish
Green and black olives for garnish
Onions for garnish

 CECILIA'S • BRECKENRIDGE, CO

Velocity Martini

1 ½ oz. Bombay Sapphire gin
Dash Martini & Rossi extra dry vermouth
Orange slice for garnish

Shake with ice, and strain into a chilled martini
glass. Serve on the rocks or straight up. Garnish
with the orange slice.

Velour Martini

1 ½ oz. Smirnoff vodka
Splash blue curaçao
Splash cranberry juice
Cranberries for garnish

Chill, and strain into a glass. Garnish with the
cranberries.

Velvet Bunny Martini

1 ½ oz. Smirnoff vodka
Dash banana liqueur
Romana Black sambuca
Banana slice for garnish

Stir with ice, and strain into a glass. Garnish with
the banana slice.

Velvet Citrus Martini

2 ½ oz. Gordon's Vodka Citrus
Lemon twist for garnish

Vendome Martini

1 oz. Beefeater gin
1 oz. Dubonnet
½ oz. dry vermouth
Lemon twist for garnish

Strain into a glass, and serve on the rocks.

Vermeer Chocolate Dream Martini

2 oz. Vermeer Dutch Chocolate Cream
1 oz. Skyy vodka
Half-and-half or milk to fill
Maraschino cherry for garnish

Shake first two ingredients well with ice. Strain into a martini glass, and fill with half-and-half. Garnish with the stemmed maraschino cherry.

 PETER O'DONNELL • SAN FRANCISCO, CA

Vermeer Chocolate Martini

2 oz. Vermeer Dutch Chocolate Cream
1 oz. Skyy vodka
Maraschino cherry for garnish

Shake well with ice, and strain into a martini glass. Garnish with the stemmed maraschino cherry.

 PETER O'DONNELL • SAN FRANCISCO, CA

Vermouth Cassis Martini

2 parts Martini & Rossi extra dry vermouth
1 part crème de cassis

Pour over ice, and stir well.

Vermouth Cocktail

1 oz. Martini & Rossi extra dry vermouth
1 oz. Martini & Rossi Rosso sweet vermouth
2 dashes orange bitters
Maraschino cherry for garnish

Stir with ice, and strain into a chilled glass.
Garnish with the maraschino cherry.

Vermouth Rinse Martini

⅛ oz. dry vermouth
2 ½ oz. Beefeater gin, chilled, to fill
Lemon twist or green olive to garnish

Coat the inside of a glass with dry vermouth.
Shake off the excess. Fill the glass with the gin.
Garnish with the lemon twist or green olive.

Vermouth Triple Sec Martini

1 oz. Bombay Sapphire gin
1 oz. Martini & Rossi extra dry vermouth
½ oz. triple sec
2 dashes orange bitters
Lemon twist for garnish

Shake with ice, and strain into a chilled martini
glass. Serve on the rocks or straight up. Garnish
with the lemon twist.

Very Berry Martini

2 oz. gin
½ oz. cranberry juice cocktail
Berry of your choice for garnish

Shake with ice, and strain into a well-chilled martini glass. Garnish with the fresh berry of your choice.

 BRIGID HECKMAN • REXVILLE, NY

Vespers

2 oz. Ketel One vodka
½ oz. Tanqueray gin
Splash Lillet

Shake with ice, and strain into a chilled martini glass. Serve on the rocks or straight up.

 LLOYD HESLIP • EMAILED TO OUR BLOG, WWW.
BARTENDERMAGAZINE.WORDPRESS.COM

Victor Martini

1 ½ oz. Martini & Rossi extra dry vermouth
½ oz. Bombay Sapphire gin
½ oz. brandy

Shake with ice, and strain into a chilled martini glass. Serve on the rocks or straight up.

Viking

2 ½ oz. Absolut Kurant vodka
½ oz. Chambord
Twist for garnish

Shake with ice, and strain into a chilled martini glass. Serve on the rocks or straight up. Garnish with the twist.

Viking Serum Martini

2 oz. Finlandia Classic vodka
½ oz. seltzer
Splash blue curaçao
Splash cranberry juice

Stir with ice, and strain into a glass on the rocks.

The Violet Hour

1 ½ oz. Sobieski vodka
½ oz. Marie Brizard Parfait Amour
Dash Anisette Marie Brizard
Orange peel for garnish

Stir all ingredients in a mixing glass with ice. Strain into a chilled martini glass. Garnish with the freshly cut orange peel.

Violetta

2 ½ oz. Absolut vodka
½ oz. blue curaçao
Splash cranberry juice
Twist for garnish

Stir. Serve on the rocks. Garnish with the twist.

VIP Martini

Dry gin to fill, chilled
Fine spray dry vermouth
Lemon twist or green olive to garnish

Fill a stemmed cocktail glass with chilled dry gin. Waft a fine spray of dry vermouth gently on the surface from an atomizer. Garnish with the lemon twist or green olive.

Visamini

1 oz. Absolut Kurant vodka
1 oz. Bacardi Limón rum
¼ oz. Midori melon liqueur
Dash Rose's Lime Juice

Serve on the rocks.

 STEVE VISAKAY • VINTAGE COCKTAIL SHAKERS

Vodka Gibson Martini

2 ½ oz. Sobieski vodka
⅛ oz. vermouth
Cocktail onions for garnish

Shake or stir. Garnish with the onion, or two or three.

Vodka Martini

2 oz. Sobieski vodka
½ oz. dry vermouth
Lemon twist or green olive for garnish

Shake with ice, and strain into a chilled martini glass. Serve on the rocks or straight up. Garnish with the twist or olive.

Voodoo Martini

2 oz. Smirnoff vodka
1 clove garlic
Lemon wedge for garnish

Chill vodka in a shaker. Thinly slice a clove of garlic, and place it at the bottom of the martini glass. Strain the vodka into the glass. Garnish with the lemon wedge.

Vuk's Martini

1 ½ oz. Baileys Irish cream
1 ½ oz. white crème de cacao
Scoop of ice cream (optional)

Shake, and serve straight up or on the rocks. The best way to have this martini is with ice cream. Put all ingredients in a blender, and whip it up.

 JOSEPH VUCKOVIC • RUSSO'S ON THE BAY • HOWARD BEACH, NY

Wai Lin Martini

2 oz. Smirnoff vodka
¼ oz. cranberry juice
¼ oz. melon liqueur
Lemon wedge for garnish

Strain, and garnish with the lemon.

Waiting for Godet Martini

2 oz. Smirnoff vodka
Dash bourbon
Dash Godet Belgian white chocolate
  liqueur
Fresh strawberry for garnish

Chill, and strain into a glass. Garnish with the fresh strawberry.

Wallet Chain

2 oz. Absolut Peppar vodka
Dash Worcestershire sauce
Splash jalapeño-stuffed olive juice
Jalapeño olives for garnish
Pearl onions for garnish

Shake with ice, and strain into a chilled martini glass. Serve on the rocks or straight up. Garnish with the jalapeño olives and pearl onions.

 JIM STACY • THE MANHATTAN CAFÉ • ATHENS, GA

Wallick Martini

1 ½ oz. Bombay Sapphire gin
Dash Hiram Walker orange curaçao
Dash Martini & Rossi extra dry vermouth
Lemon twist or olives for garnish

Stir with ice, and strain into a glass. Serve straight up or on the rocks. Garnish with the lemon twist or olives.

Walter Martini

2 oz. Bombay Sapphire gin
½ oz. dry sherry
½ oz. dry vermouth
2 drops lemon juice

Shake with ice, and strain into a chilled martini glass. Serve on the rocks or straight up.

Warden Martini

1 ½ oz. Bombay Sapphire gin
Dash Martini & Rossi extra dry vermouth
Dash Pernod
Lemon twist or olives for garnish

Stir with ice, and strain into a chilled martini glass. Serve on the rocks or straight up. Garnish with the lemon twist or olives.

Watermelon Martini

3 oz. watermelon juice
2 oz. Absolut Citron vodka
Splash Rose's Lime Juice

Shake vigorously with ice, and strain into a chilled martini glass.

Watermelon Martini II

5 oz. Grey Goose vodka
½ oz. cranberry juice
½ oz. sour mix

Shake with ice, and strain into a chilled martini glass. Serve on the rocks or straight up.

Wayne's Martini

3 oz. Beefeater gin
⅛ oz. Glen Ord single malt scotch whiskey
2 green olives stuffed with anchovy for
   garnish

Stir gently over cracked ice, and strain into a chilled 5-oz. martini glass. Garnish with 2 green olives stuffed with anchovy.

 WAYNE BECKWITH • FAIRPORT VILLAGE INN • FAIRPORT, NY

Well, What the People Think Are Martinis!

1 ¼ oz. Grand Marnier
1 oz. Absolut vodka
1 oz. Bombay Sapphire gin
1 oz. cranberry juice
⅝ oz. freshly squeezed lemon juice
¼-inch lemon wheel caramelized with
    sugar for garnish

Chill in a shaker, and serve straight up in a chilled martini glass. Garnish with the lemon wheel.

 DARYLE NORBERG, BARTENDER • BYRON'S SPORTS BAR • SAN LEANDRO, CA

Wembley Martini

1 ½ oz. dry gin
¾ oz. dry vermouth
¼ oz. apple brandy
Dash apricot-flavored brandy

Shake with ice, and strain into a chilled martini glass. Serve on the rocks or straight up.

West Peachtree Martini

2 ½ oz. Stolichnaya Peachik vodka
⅛ oz. cranberry juice

Shake with ice, and strain into a chilled martini glass. Serve on the rocks or straight up.

 RENAISSANCE ATLANTA HOTEL • ATLANTA, GA

White Chocolate Martini

Chocolate shell to rim
1 ½ oz. Skyy vodka
½ oz. Godiva white chocolate liqueur
Hershey's Hug for garnish

Chill a glass, and rim it with chocolate shell. Shake ingredients, and pour into the chilled glass. Garnish with the Hershey's Hug candy.

 PAMELA CONAWAY • HURRICANE RESTAURANT
• PASSAGRILLE, FL

White Chocolate Martini II

2 ½ oz. Grey Goose La Vanille
¼ oz. Frangelico
¼ oz. Godiva white chocolate liqueur
¼ oz. white crème de cacao

Shake with ice, and strain into a chilled martini glass. Serve on the rocks or straight up.

 FLEUR DE LYS • MANDALAY BAY • LAS VEGAS, NV

White Lady

1 ½ oz. gin
¾ oz. Cointreau
⅓ oz. lemon juice

Shake with ice, and strain into a martini glass.

 REMY AMERIQUE, INC. • NEW YORK, NY

White Russian Martini

2 oz. Smirnoff vodka
1 oz. half-and-half
1 oz. Kahlúa

Combine. Strain into a chilled martini glass.

White Way Cocktail Martini

1 ½ oz. Beefeater gin
¾ oz. white crème de menthe

Shake with cracked ice, and strain into a chilled glass.

Why Not Martini

1 oz. apricot brandy
1 oz. Beefeater gin
1 tsp. lemon juice
Lemon twist for garnish

Shake with ice, and strain into a glass. Garnish with the lemon twist.

Wild Horse

1 ½ oz. Stolichnaya Razberi vodka
½ oz. amaretto
Fresh raspberry for garnish

Serve chilled in a martini glass. Garnish with the fresh raspberry.

 IFIS VOURLATOS • EMAILED TO OUR BLOG, WWW. BARTENDERMAGAZINE.WORDPRESS.COM

Wild Rose Martini

1 ½ oz. dry gin
½ oz. dry vermouth
½ oz. sweet vermouth
Dash Angostura bitters
Dash orange bitters

Shake with ice, and strain into a chilled martini glass. Serve on the rocks or straight up.

Will Rogers Martini

1 ½ oz. gin
½ oz. dry vermouth
½ oz. orange juice
¼ oz. triple sec

Shake with ice, and strain into a chilled glass.

Wilson Special Martini

2 oz. Bombay Sapphire gin
¼ oz. Martini & Rossi extra dry vermouth
2 orange slices for garnish

Shake, and garnish with the orange slices.

Windex Martini

Lemon to rim
Sugar to rim
1 oz. 7-Up
1 oz. Ketel One vodka
1 oz. sour mix
½ oz. Cointreau
Maraschino cherry for garnish

Rim a glass with the lemon and sugar. Shake well, strain, and garnish with the maraschino cherry.

 LISA MCARTHUR, CHEERLEADERS •
PHILADELPHIA, PA

Windex Martini II

2 ½ oz. vodka
2 oz. lemonade
½ oz. blue curaçao

Shake, and serve with a strainer and martini glass.

Windsock Martini

2 oz Absolut Kurant vodka
¼ oz. cranberry juice
¼ oz. lemon juice
Lemon peel for garnish

Shake with ice, and strain into a chilled martini glass. Serve on the rocks or straight up. Garnish with the lemon peel.

 THE WINDSOCK BAR & GRILL • SAN DIEGO, CA

Woodford Pumpkin Pie Martini

1 ¼ oz. Woodford Reserve bourbon
¾ oz. pumpkin liqueur
Splash amaretto
Dab fresh whipped cream
Dust nutmeg
Sprinkle pie crumbs
Cinnamon stick for garnish

Combine Woodford Reserve, pumpkin liqueur, and amaretto in a shaker filled with ice. Shake, and strain into a chilled martini glass. Top with whipped cream, nutmeg, and pie crumbs. Garnish with the cinnamon stick.

 W. ROSE • LOUISVILLE, KY

Xanthia Martini

1 ½ oz. dry gin
1 oz. Cointreau
1 oz. dry vermouth

Mix, and serve on the rocks.

X-Boyfriend

2 ½ oz. X-Rated Fusion liqueur
¼ oz. fresh lime juice
Seltzer to top

Shake first two ingredients. Serve in a martini glass. Top with seltzer.

 RAYMOND AUBEL • VICEROY • NEW YORK, NY

Yachting Club Martini

1 ¾ oz. Holland's gin
¾ oz. dry vermouth
2 dashes Peychaud's bitters
Dash Pernod
Sugar to taste

Mix the first four ingredients. Sweeten with sugar to taste.

Yachting Martini

1 ½ oz. Smirnoff vodka
⅛ oz. Midori melon liqueur
⅛ oz. peach schnapps
Peach wedge for garnish

Chill, and strain into a glass. Garnish with the fresh peach wedge.

Yale Cocktail Martini

1 ½ oz. Beefeater gin
½ oz. Martini & Rossi extra dry vermouth
1 tsp. blue curaçao or cherry brandy
Dash bitters

Stir, and serve on the rocks.

Yale Martini

1 ⅔ oz. Plymouth gin
½ oz. dry vermouth
¼ oz. maraschino cherry juice
2 dashes orange bitters
Sugar to taste

Mix the first four ingredients. Sweeten with sugar to taste.

Yang Martini

2 ½ oz. gin
½ oz. sake

Stir with ice, and strain into a chilled martini glass.

 INAGIKU • NEW YORK, NY

Yellow Daisy

1 ½ oz. Beefeater gin
½ oz. dry vermouth
¼ oz. Grand Marnier
¼ oz. Pernod
Maraschino cherry for garnish

Shake with ice, and strain into a chilled martini
glass. Serve on the rocks or straight up.

Yellow Fingers Martini

1 ½ oz. gin
¾ oz. blackberry brandy
½ oz. cream
½ oz. crème de bananes

Shake with ice, and strain into a chilled glass.

Yellow Rattler

2 oz. Bombay Sapphire gin
1 oz. extra dry vermouth
Dash orange bitters
2 cocktail onions for garnish

Shake with ice, and strain into a chilled martini glass. Serve on the rocks or straight up. Garnish with the cocktail onions.

Ying Martini

2 ½ oz. sake
½ oz. gin

Stir with ice, and strain into a chilled martini glass.

 INAGIKU • NEW YORK, NY

Yolanda Martini

¾ oz. brandy
¾ oz. dry gin
½ oz. sweet vermouth
¼ oz. grenadine
¼ oz. Pernod

Stir. Serve on the rocks.

Yukon Martini

Dash Yukon Jack
2 oz. Smirnoff vodka
Lemon wedge for garnish

Coat a martini glass with Yukon Jack. Chill, and strain vodka into the martini glass. Garnish with the lemon wedge.

Zanzibar Martini

2 ½ oz. dry vermouth
1 oz. gin
½ oz. lemon juice
1 tsp. sugar syrup
3 dashes bitters
Lemon twist for garnish

Stir with ice, and strain into a glass. Garnish with the lemon twist.

Zinamartini

¼ oz. dry vermouth
1 ½ oz. Stolichnaya Zinamon vodka
Cinnamon stick for garnish

Pour vermouth into a martini glass. Discard vermouth, and add vodka. Garnish with the cinnamon stick.

 JOE CHIRONNO • CELEBRITY PUB • WHEATLEY HEIGHTS, NY

Zorbatini Martini

1 ½ oz. Stolichnaya vodka
¼ oz. Metaxa ouzo
Green olive for garnish

Stir gently with ice, and strain. Garnish with the green olive.

YOUR MARTINI RECIPES

DRINK INDEX

469

R

S

ALCOHOL INDEX

490

W

X

ABOUT THE AUTHOR

Ray Foley, a former marine with over thirty years of bartending and restaurant experience, is the founder and editor of *Bartender Magazine*. Ray is referred to as "The Legend" for all he has done for bartenders and bartending. *Bartender Magazine* is the only magazine in the world specifically geared toward bartenders and the on-premise and is one of the very few primarily designed for servers of alcohol. *Bartender Magazine* is enjoying its thirty-first year and currently has a circulation of OVER one hundred thousand and is steadily growing.

After serving in the United States Marine Corps and attending Seton Hall University, Ray entered the restaurant business as a bartender, which eventually led to a job as the assistant general manager of The Manor in West Orange, New Jersey, with over 350 employees.

In 1983, Ray left The Manor to devote his full efforts to *Bartender Magazine*. The circulation and exposure has grown from seven thousand to over one hundred thousand to date and has become the largest on-premise liquor magazine in the country.

Ray has been published in numerous articles throughout the country and has appeared on many TV and radio shows.

He is the founder of the Bartender Hall of Fame, which honors the best bartenders throughout the United States, not only for their abilities at bartending but for their involvement and service in their communities as well.

Ray is also the founder of The Bartenders' Foundation Incorporated. This nonprofit foundation has been set up to raise scholarship money for bartenders and their families. Scholarships awarded to bartenders can be used to either further their education or can go toward the education of their children.

Ray is the founder of www.bartender.com (over 1.5 million hits per month) and www.USBartender.com, and many other bar-related websites.

Mr. Foley serves as a consultant to some of our nation's foremost distillers and importers. He is also responsible for naming and creating new drinks for the liquor industry. Here are just a few:

"The Fuzzy Navel"
"The Royal Stretch"—for Grand Royal Oaks Race
"The Royal Turf"—for Grand Royal Oaks Race
"Pink Cadillac"

"Pear-A-Terre"
"Grapeful Red"
"Pear A Mud"
"Pearsian Kat"
"Pomtree Cocktail"
"The Royal Sour"
"The Hamptons "Golden Apfel"
"Mosquito Bite"

Ray has one of the largest collections of cocktail recipe books in the world, dating back to the 1800s and is one of the foremost collectors of cocktail shakers, having 368 shakers in his collection.

He is the author of the following bestsellers:

Bartending for Dummies
Running a Bar for Dummies
The Ultimate Cocktail Book
The Ultimate Little Shooter Book
The Ultimate Little Martini Book
The Ultimate Little Blender Book
Advice from Anonymous
The Best Irish Drinks
Jokes, Quotes and Bartoons
Beer is the Answer...What is the Question?
X-Rated Drinks
Bartender Magazine's Ultimate Bartender's Guide
Vodka 1000
Rum 1000
Tequila 1000
The Best Summer Drinks
God Loves Golfers Best

Ray resides in New Jersey with his wife and partner of 28 years, Jackie, and their son, Ryan.

For additional information or a media kit, please contact:

Jaclyn Foley, Publisher of
Bartender Magazine
Foley Publishing Corporation
PO Box 158, Liberty Corner, NJ 07938
Telephone: (908) 766-6006
Fax: (908) 766-6607
Email: BarMag@aol.com
Website: www.Bartender.com